TWO TO TANGO

TWO TO TANGO

Choreographies for a Challenging Love

SUSANA BALÁN

To order additional copies of this book, contact:
Xlibris Corporation
1-888-795-4274
www.Xlibris.com
Orders@Xlibris.com
25197

Contents

IN MEMORIAM

Socorro Soberón, who wrote to her granddaughter:

"Una cosa parecida me pasó a mí con mi mamá, y dice tu mamá que ella está dispuesta a pasarla conmigo, cosa que no creo que ocurra porque yo no quiero, ¿sabes? . . . La cadena tiene que romperse en algún lado, en algún momento, espero que ese momento y ese lugar sea éste . . . Por primera vez conmigo existe la familia de pareja . . ." (México, 1996)

and Viola Sheely, who wrote me:

"The true challenge today in a relationship is letting go of old habits. Creating a new kind of love different from our parents. It felt so real[. . .]. I feel this was truly a new beginning for my husband and I." (Bali, 1998)

What is a story if not a metaphor, a myth in the making? Love is a raft in a swiftly moving river, scant protection against rapids and rocks, a private place of smells and tastes, eloquences looks and intimate touch, a cache of common dreams and accumulated history. We seek its secret, but it is as individual as one's own face, hidden even form ourselves. Me, Joan; you, Al. We have conceptual differences. We *are* conceptual differences. We don't even pull into the driveway the same way. But isn't that where love begins, in the differences-the otherness-that makes love possible, and necessary? Love is the mystery of union, the distance to be transcended, the fuel to cross an infinity. It's another kind of math. Two times Love equals One. We are One and not One, a paradox in being. And that's only the half of it, maybe only half of the half of the half—my half. We shout and we shut up. We laugh, we paddle. The fuel is a flame that flickers. We give it air, and we trust the flame will not go out. The dramatic tension is internal.

Joan Konner

El baile del tango es la búsqueda del hombre y la mujer. Es la búsqueda del abrazo. Es la forma de estar juntos y de que el hombre se sienta hombre y la mujer, mujer, sin machismo. A la mujer le gusta ser llevada y al hombre le gusta llevar. Despúes vendrán los problemas o no, pero en este momento es importante llegar a un diálogo progresivo y positivo, al cincuenta por ciento. La música motiva y angustia, el baile es la unión de dos personas indefensas frente al mundo y a la impotencia de cambiar las cosas.

Juan Carlos Copes

Mother, I conquered the world for you. You were the Mother I needed. I'm a fighter. What would I have done with a Mother who smothered me in love? [. . . .] Thank you Mother. What a boring life I would have had without you.

Niki de Saint Phalle

You cannot be syncretic easily. It's dangerous. It's exciting, too, but being both syncretic and eclectic can be very dangerous because creating, performing, composing, these things demand focus and concentration, and also truth in perspective.[. . .] It is the era of comparisons, that you can put things side by side and suggest surprising comparisons that will change your way of thinking and feeling.

Caetano Veloso

INTRODUCTION

"We learned from women your age how to fight but not how to love": with a voice saddened by her repeated romantic failures said Lena, a successful Mexican journalist. Defining herself as a faithful representative of the so-called "Generation X"-to which my daughters also belong—Lena tried to explain to me why she refused to accept the idea that she and her peers were, as their mothers seemed to believe, either "ingenuous who still believe in fairy tales" or "so bad and selfish that no man will have us."

She insisted: "We learned from you how to flourish professionally but not personally. We learned from you how to work but not how to nurture. We learned from you how to argue but not how to agree. First, our mothers taught us to want it all. They told us that we deserved the best. But when we want to find a person who understands us and complements us in every way, they criticize us and tell us that we are too ambitious and that in life one must compromise. They don't accept any responsibility for this state of affairs. They made us think that if we liberated ourselves from dependence on men, we would be happy, but they don't see that they were wrong. Liberty has not brought us greater happiness. Either this recipe doesn't work or never worked, or they forgot to let us in on some secret." This conversation took place some time ago during my first year of professional life in New York.

Some weeks later, Alessandra, a beautiful Italian lawyer, surrounded by consultants, friends and relatives who adore her, wanted to know if I could explain to her why she and other women like her—supremely successful in many parts of life—fell in love with men who mistreated them and became bored with those who treated them well.

"Is it wrong to want more? Why can't I aspire to everything? If I'm ambitious and demand the most of myself in every aspect of my life, why can't I demand the most of myself in my love life and find what I most want, a man both powerful and good?" She asked herself.

Her father's advice, that love was like a hunt with hunters and prey, did not satisfy her. She did not want to hunt (and mistreat the man who loved her) nor did she want to be hunted (and be mistreated by the man she loved.)

My explanations, similar to her mother's, did not satisfy her either. I told her to be "more tolerant," advice she found unacceptable. She did not want a romantic partner whom she had to care for as if he were a stupid child. Her friends' suggestions, that she conform more, did not sit well with her personal style. It's true that she did not need by her side a man who would care for her as if she were a little girl, it's true that she was completely independent and able to resolve all her life issues on her own, but, exactly for this reason, she wanted a companion who knew more than she did, from whom she could continue to learn.

In these same months of 1999, I suffered through endless arguments accompanying the preparations for my daughter Natasha's wedding. Born in Buenos Aires in 1970, Natasha was the child of an agnostic and long-divorced couple, of a father from the city raised by a Catholic mother of Italian descent and a Masonic father of French descent, of a mother (me) from the provinces, raised by a couple of Russian-Jewish origin that had adopted the *gaucho* traditions of their birthplace.

Until that time, I'd thought that Natasha's romantic troubles came from her cultural and religious syncretism, her various migrations—from the Buenos Aires of her birth to the Rio de Janeiro of her childhood to the Buenos Aires of her adolescence to the Toronto of her young adulthood where she still lives. She confirmed my fears when she began her adolescence suffering because she didn't fit in completely to any group, any religion or any age. She complained because she didn't know whether her 'real' friends were those who stayed in Buenos Aires, where she had lived for only six of her twelve years, the daughters of my Brazilian friends, her classmates or the neighbors whom she played with in Rio de Janeiro. She complained because she didn't know whether to calm her anguish by reciting the Lord's prayer, as her Catholic paternal grandmother recommended, or by asking for forgiveness and correcting her errors as the ethical rules of her Jewish maternal grandmother suggested, or by trusting some *macumba* and obeying local rites of *candomblé*, as her Brazilian nanny did. She complained because she didn't know whether it would be more enjoyable to stay home playing dolls with her friends and younger sister or going out dancing with her older cousin and the cousin's grown-up boyfriend. She could pass through various places but she never fit in entirely or "for always," as she used to say inconsolably.

Her primary anger was directed at me, because, as her mother—her matrix, her origin and point of departure—I didn't offer her an integrated home for all her beings and doings. I didn't offer her a precise embrace. I could teach her Israeli dances but not Brazilian ones, I could explain how she should behave at the Teatro Municipal where I brought her to see the ballets that enchanted her, but I quaked with fear when her father taught her how to jump waves at the often too rough sea at Ipanema. I could help her with her social studies homework, but I cried with her when I couldn't understand mathematics. Her father, her grandmothers, her nanny, her friends and I could offer her names for some of her ideas, emotions and customs but not for others. Natasha could not define herself fully, could not be named by a single word, or confined to a single emotion, idea or custom. She saw herself as foreign and 'strange,' in all languages, geographies and customs that she inhabited nevertheless as if she were a native citizen thereof.

During her youth, her romantic relationships showed the same lack of fit. If I was delighted by the "o namorado que a mae quer" (the boyfriend that mothers want), as she introduced one of her boyfriends to me, she discovered after several years that he was too cautious and didn't understand her need to dance until dawn. If I managed to understand the virtues of the boyfriend who was interesting as a person but not adequate as the future father of my grandchildren, she discovered, after having incorporated him successfully into our family rituals, that he was too reckless and didn't understand her interest in the pleasures of middle-class life or in classical music. The four candidates who took up the ten years prior to her meeting Carlos—the young Canadian of Portuguese Catholic origin whom she would marry the following year—had loved her, had wanted to marry her and start a family with her. With effort in some cases, with ease in others, the four had been able to count on my approval. But not on Natasha's. After a time, generally corresponding to the time it took me to develop affection for, accept and appreciate the reasons Natasha had chosen as she had, she would decide that the current candidate was not the man for her. One offered her an overly bohemian embrace, another was too structured, one was too passionate, another too rational. One was too strong, another to weak. With each of them, Natasha had radiated happiness as long as they shared the same way of looking at the world; but she became angry and sad when she had to accept that differing points of view made a daily life together impossible. Each candidate embraced her easily and lightly in some ways, stiflingly in others. I liked one boyfriend, her father, another. Her Brazilian friends liked the one disliked by her Argentine friends and vice-versa. With one she went to elegant restaurants dressed in handmade t-shirts and sandals and with another she spent long early mornings drinking gin and coffee in silk shirts she had stolen from my closet.

But my consultants, who also complained of not fitting in completely to any embrace and of not meeting the right man, had been born and raised in the bosom of families that were geographically, socially, religiously and culturally homogenous. Their parents hadn't divorced when they were little; they had not changed geography, language, color, scent or taste repeatedly as my own daughters had. They were univocally and homogenously French or Brazilian or American or Indian or German or Argentine. Their families of origin were univocally and homogenously middle—or upper-class, liberal professionals or intellectuals or artists. Some continued practicing the creed with which they were raised, and they were univocally Catholic, Jewish, Protestant, Hindu, agnostic or atheist. Unlike my daughters, these women were not the result of religious or cultural or linguistic or social syncretisms. But their emotional background was the same: all inherited an emotional legacy that required them to sift through contradictory meanings of what it meant to be 'strong,' 'weak,' 'good,' or 'bad.' Because of this contradictory legacy, they cannot fit into any of the above categories.

They shared with my daughters the feeling of being 'strange' or different, not culturally but emotionally, from any group of women their age: they did not fit in to the housewife group or the executive group, but they were excellent hostesses and excellent professionals. They were neither tender nor hard, but they knew themselves as extremely sensitive and extremely efficient; neither rational nor irrational, but able to sustain both rigorous logic and illogical intuition; neither predictable nor unpredictable, but proper in their fulfillments of commitments and extravagant in their ability to surprise. Sometimes they felt themselves to be too good, sometimes too bad; sometimes they felt weaker than other women, sometimes stronger than some men. Sometimes they felt better than and sometimes worse than the majority of people. From an emotional point of view, my consultants, like my daughters, felt that they were nobody and nothing. And all shared the feeling of being misunderstood by their mothers and by the men they loved; a lack of understanding that was not explained by differences in cultural or religious or gender languages.

Given that my consultants loved their mothers (who did not feel loved by them) and that I loved my daughters (who did not feel loved by me), I began to believe that a grave misunderstanding was circulating among us all.

During this time, some of my consultants were men, also of my daughters' generation, who complained of women: "I don't understand them; I don't know what they want;" "They make me crazy, their moods change all the time, they always want something different from what they've just requested." These men thought that their girlfriends were marvelous, but so incomprehensible that they ended by sapping their strength entirely and boring them.

I became even more worried: I had always feared (and I know that my consultants' mothers also feared) that no man could truly approach my daughters if they kept acting as they had since they were born, as if they were wild indomitable horses, insatiable in their desires to love everything, do everything, see everything.

But Natasha showed me that I was wrong: Carlos understood her and wanted to marry her precisely because both shared the desire for excellence in their emotional lives, an excellence they already know how to strive for in other areas of life. Borrowing the words of the poet Fernando Pessoa, they announced their wedding by inviting guests to "Navegar é preciso, viver não é preciso" (Better to sail and not to live than live and not to sail). Both had felt strange and different from the majority of their peers, as regards their emotional needs, but they had found each other. And they celebrated the precise, exact, necessary, specific and unique embrace that each promised to give the other.

I began to think that Lena was right: some women of my generation had taught our daughters to love as we did, teachings that, in the new world in which they live, do not do them any good.

Perhaps the emotional miss-encounters between mothers and daughters and between women and men were not due to lack of love but to the lack of system of simultaneous translation between our different emotional languages. Perhaps my daughters' 'strange' way of loving was the external manifestation of a rupture: a drastic and definitive change as much with their grandmothers' emotional model as with their mothers'. Perhaps these 'strange' women showed characteristics of a mutation in emotional being and could therefore show the rest of us a new way of loving.

For women of my grandmother's generation, the world was a world of men. Women were and behaved like Adam's rib, as if they were part of the men to whom they belonged. For my mother's generation, the world was divided into two halves, the public and the private, men's and women's, the king's and the queen's—each gender reined in its own partial sphere. In my generation, some women and some men wanted to migrate to the other kingdom; we did so, but we kept one leg in each world. By doing so, we often felt as if we were being drawn and quartered. In my daughters' generation, some men and women seem to suffer greatly because they neither want to be quartered as their parents were nor to return to the divided worlds of their grandparents. And I have observed that some of these women and men, in their efforts to find a way out of their suffering, have created a new way of being. Syncretically, sifting through emotional legacies, they learn how to dance with the other in a very specific way. How? They neither erase nor exaggerate the difference between men and women. Instead, by incorporating the emotional linguistic differences into themselves, they recognize that they must seek a translation of the other's emotional signals.

With this hypothesis in mind, and in my heart, I dedicated myself to observing more carefully which manner of loving did work for them; which way worked for the men who understood them, which for the women and their mothers. And, with the generous participation of some of these women and men I began to notice certain repeated behaviors that didn't seem to be due to personal or individual characteristics. Among the women and men, with me acting as a virtual translator (because these people rarely met in person), we discovered that some women and men formed part of a larger collectivity, until now not recognized as such. They had not met because—ignorant of the existence of others like themselves—they had not known how to recognize one another.

This book aims to be a kind of collective notebook of the romantic journey of the women (the men's book has not yet been written) who belong to this collectivity, small in number but recognizable in their specific forms.

In the first chapters I describe the vocabularies and models of love that I inherited from my grandparents and parents. In following ones, I show how some women and men of my daughters' generation use and reinvent our teachings, both explicit and implicit. Bridging past and present, personal narrative and social narrative, and self and society are the figures of my daughters themselves, and of the various shapes they and I have made as we try to work out a new mode of loving both ourselves and others. I bolster my arguments upon three metaphors, that of the embrace, the dance, and the figure of the syncrete.

To embrace, says the dictionary, is to stretch between or tighten with the arms. In a broader sense, this word is also used to talk about the idea of understanding, inclusion, admitting, receiving, to be in favor, to follow, to take something into one's care and take care of it. Metaphorically, I describe precise and imprecise forms, divided and shared, benefits and drawbacks, of embracing-understanding-taking care of a person.

To dance means to execute rhythmic movements. Partner dances require, additionally, that such movements are coordinated not only with music but also between the dancers. Metaphorically, I describe happy and unhappy ways for coordinating movements between members of different types of couples.

Syncretism, the dictionary also informs us, refers to the result of attempting to harmonize elements of different origins. Generally, it is used to name religions or new syncretic cultures, formed from a combination of elements of two or more religions or traditional cultures. Metaphorically, I speak of syncretic emotionality to refer to the original ways in which some people of my daughters' generation sift and rearrange the emotional legacies received from past generations. I avoid resorting to the word "hybrid," used in an equivalent way, because of the indefinite connotation to which this term alludes.

While the information I summarize here is primarily based on data given me by successful professionals of both sexes, heterosexual and homosexual, between thirty and forty years old, Americans and those of other nationalities, resident in New York, I limit myself to speaking of heterosexual women who, following a path full of trials and errors, knew how to transform the pains of this search for love into wisdom and, ultimately, how to find the love they sought.

All came to New York in search of better professional opportunities and with the secret desire to meet, in this tremendous city, a man who would offer them a tremendous, different, nearly impossible to imagine embrace.

Despite my infinite need to stop and renounce this project, which often struck me as pointless, I followed my literary path in much the same way as my daughters and consultants continued— long after many of their peers had stopped, exhausted by turbulence and uncertainty—the search for the romantic port that would provide them with a safe haven. Repeating the vicissitudes of their travels I, like them, many times thought I had arrived only to discover with unspeakable pain that I had merely come to a rock on which it was impossible to disembark, or that the land which seemed firm and pleasant was full of enemies waiting to attack me with pitiless violence. (My critical sense told me that not even I myself understood what I had written.)

I rewrote every chapter hundreds of times: I gathered more information as I did so and, after re-reading, found that the chapters made no sense if they did not integrate all the information into a unifying whole.

Encounters as precise as those of Natasha and Carlos, in which ended some of my consultants' romantic journeys, let me arrive at the final version of the book.

Many anecdotes which I did not know how to incorporate have been left out. But my gratitude to my daughters and my consultants and for all I learned from them infuses every word in this book.

Chapters 1-4 tell of my own travels in the world of the emotions, a journey which begins with my mother still in her own mother's womb and ends with my daughters already born. Chapters 5-8 tell of the travels of women my daughters' age and of their survival strategies developed to deal with their mothers' emotional contradictions. Chapters 9 and 10 tell of the newly charted romantic course of some of these women. And Chapter 11 details the logistics of the steps of this new way of navigating romantic love.

Acknowledgments of and thanks for specific people and books finish the book's passage.

New York, 2004

1

A Saga of Family Embraces

My grandmother Rosa, my mother's mother, was fourteen when she came to Argentina at the start of 1904, fleeing the persecution of the Jews in her native Russia. Her family could only afford to pay for two people's passage: she and her older sister were picked to elude death and to begin a new life in a land that appeared as promising as it was mysterious and far away. The sisters were expelled for protection, uprooted for love. They obeyed weeping. They were scared to leave the familiar and to confront the unknown. They felt guilty for betraying their loved ones in order to survive. They felt angry and powerless before the great abundance of their new world, an abundance they would be unable to share. These emotions wouldn't leave them even when their great relief at their own survival allowed them to smile again; they would never again laugh as children laugh, fully and freely.

My grandmother's dowry consisted of a scrap of paper on which was written and partially erased the name of José, who had left her village the year before. When my grandmother went in search of him, he was already a man of twenty-seven. He was understood to be living in northern Argentina, in a farming community established by Jews from various parts of Central Europe. If he came from a family of small businessmen and knew nothing about farming or about the country, my grandmother's family nevertheless imagined him as successful in the new enterprise. And so Rosa was supposed to meet him and marry him. She was to survive, putting down roots in the promised land, extend her own life through that of her family, and fill with new images her now-emptied memory.

My grandmother didn't seek the perfect encounter, a total or true love. These hopes were not part of the repertoire of possible affects for women such as herself, immigrants without family resources. She wanted a husband who would allow her to maintain herself and to extend life through her children, following as she did the mandate she had received from her mother. She neither chose her husband nor looked for a husband to love. These needs were far from her thoughts and even farther from her imagination. She committed herself, without question, to the life of a procreative wife. She needed merely to meet and marry a man who would fulfill his marital duties effectively by protecting her and her children. This is all that, for her, marriage meant. Rosa met José, made herself his bride of choice, and married him; they would go on to have seven children.

They never loved each other in the sense of feeling attracted by or to each other—such is the dictionary's definition of love— but they overcame, together and with their family, ecological and bureaucratic disasters during their first years in the new land. These shared experiences solidified their union, which lasted until José's death after more than fifty years. My grandmother counted herself fortunate because, in addition to guaranteeing her shelter, food and social legitimacy, her husband shared with her memories of snow, songs, food, religious customs, a certain idea of home and her native language. Between them there were no games of seduction, no overpowering passions, no profound looks or intimate discoveries. They did what they had to do: he provided economic sustenance and social integration of the family into the community; she took care of the children and of the domestic sphere.

My grandmother always considered herself a weak person and she acted accordingly. It was not she who decided to leave her family in the old world; it was not she who decided which man to marry, where to live, when or how many children to bring into the world. She was a wife: as such she must define herself; that was her identity. She had a husband who took care of the material needs of herself and her family: what more could she want? If she did want something else, something outside the desires proscribed for her as wife and mother, she had to devise ingenious means to force her husband to permit her to have what she wanted.

My grandmother was an expert at survival. She overcame risks of death, hunger, bodily punishments and the deprivations of an unknown land. She also overcame the constant lack of attention to her desires that was part of her marriage. For Rosa always wanted something more than physical survival, enough food, and shelter from the elements. She wanted to live well. She wanted to take part in cultural life; she hungered for something more than the bare bones of survival. And, from her subordinate position, she acquired some of what she wanted. She learned how to convince her strong husband, owner of the decision-making power, of the extent to which he needed what she wanted. This was not so difficult: she thought of herself as part of her husband, as if her existence were limited to the role she played in her husband's family.

Water was scarce in this region and my grandfather needed it to grow the alfalfa he sold to the landowners of the area. It never would have crossed his mind to use something so necessary for money-making on something as unnecessary as he felt my grandmother's hoped-for garden to be. But my grandmother ensured that the roses, lilies, daisies, and snapdragons so needed to feed her soul, got as much or more care as the alfalfa. My grandmother's flowers never lacked water. If my grandfather didn't provide it—already convinced by my grandmother that he needed the miracle of blossoming flowers in those desolate fields—his sons would, trying thereby to combat their mother's painful depressions, long periods of silence, or absent gazes.

My grandmother's melancholy wasn't sham, a strategy for getting what she wanted. Her sufferings were real, as were her weaknesses and her lack of economic and social resources. Sadness, passivity, and dependency comprised her only property, formed part of her capital. My grandmother learned how to use these things as defensive arms: she turned them into the force of the weak. It would never have crossed her mind to feel badly about manipulating her husband in order to get what she wanted. She did so in order for the person-Rosa to survive hidden in the clothing of the mother-Rosa and wife-Rosa.

My grandfather took himself to be satisfied with being alive, hearing the birds sing as evening fell on the Argentine plains, far from the dangers of the Siberian steppes. He hummed nostalgically ballads from his childhood as he traveled the countryside on horseback, and he remembered his father's face as he repeated a ritual he'd learned with him: sipping tea through a sugar cube he held between his teeth even on the most broiling of summer days. By contrast, my grandmother always wanted something more than to feel herself free of the persecutions of her native land. She wanted to inhabit her new country, to master its landscapes, its customs, its foods and its scents. She did not manage to do so entirely. She remained Russian, an immigrant woman who spoke Spanish with a strange accent. But she encouraged her children to adopt fully the customs of their home. She wanted her children to feel and to act like full citizens of the new world, to help her forget the ancestral terrors that plagued her memories still. Out of her love for them grew her desire that they differentiate themselves from her. She accepted the risk of their becoming strange to her, of their inhabiting a different cultural territory.

I suppose that the origins of my interest in psychology stem from the trips my grandmother took to Buenos Aires in the fifties as a patient of the first psychoanalysts in the country. My mother, her eldest daughter, always went with her. The big city was very far away from their village; in it, far from my grandfather's control, Rosa took Spanish classes, went to the theater, and went to pastry shops for sweets her husband would have found superfluous. But the pastries tasted of pleasures stolen, ephemeral and incomplete. She allowed herself to have them as an antidote to depression, but she couldn't enjoy them as a life pleasure.

My mother and others of her generation felt estranged from themselves when they began their cultural migration and learned the customs, the language, the values, and the ways of thinking and feeling of the natives of their new land. For a long time, they didn't fit in to either of their two territories: neither in to the local gaucho traditions nor in to the orthodox Jewish traditions of their ancestors. My aunt Clara, who always helped me understand various family codes, to listen to what went unsaid and to see what remained hidden, suffered because she wanted to belong to the tennis club that her friends were members of. Her parents didn't allow her to join because the members were *goyim* rather than Jews and they worried that she would fall in love with someone and abandon her traditions. But at the same time they encouraged her to continue her studies far from the small village in which they lived, far from the control of the inward-looking Jewish community—running the same risk from which at times they fled. Clara felt ill at ease in both groups, but she ended up more at home among the gauchos. My mother, equally ill at ease, felt more at home among the immigrant Jews who made up her parents' circle. She recalled sadly a childhood anecdote: a classmate, the daughter of Spanish immigrants, made the sign of the cross screaming "the devil, the devil" when learning that my mother was Jewish.

Clara, my mother, and others from this second generation of Jewish immigrants in Argentina found themselves mistrusted as much by the local gauchos as by the first generation of immigrant Jews. Some mistrusted them because they acted *gaucha* but in an unusual way; they were attacked then by people who felt invaded by others both recognizable and foreign. Some mistrusted them because they acted like Jews without respecting strictly the traditional customs; they were then accused of being renegades, of betraying those to whom they were foreign but recognizable.

Some of these creatures, lugging their confused cultural baggage behind them, chose to assimilate completely, thereby avoiding attacks from the natives. They changed their last names, they forgot Yiddish, they forgot their traditional customs and values. They dressed as *gauchos* and they killed their own pasts. Others chose to maintain their religious and familiar customs without any changes, thereby avoiding being called traitors. They negated the passage of time, the dizzying changes in geography through which they had lived. They never entered their present, nor inhabited culturally their new land.

But there were others who survived the fear of being rejected by some people and abandoned by others. People such as my aunt, my mother and my father learned to tolerate equally the rage of not being well-accepted by the locals and the guilt of having abandoned the immigrants. They learned to defend themselves without counterattacking the natives or betraying their own. They pushed themselves to break the chain of mandated repetition of custom and tradition and they invented, from their divided cultures, a conjoined culture, a hyphenated identity: that of Argentine *gaucho-judío*.

This complexity invented a new way of being. They spoke Yiddish and Spanish: the language of their parents and of their natal land. They knew the sound of *balalaikas* and guitars, the laments of Russian songs and of *vidalas*. They cooked both borscht and *empanadas*. They loved the unconditional solidarity of their family belonging and the indomitable liberty of the prairie solitude. Speech and silence, tradition and creativity, the old and the new, the known and the unknown, the integration into a group and the individual self, faith in Jehovah and faith in *Pachamama*: thus they knit together the skein of this new identity.

The Argentine Jewish *gauchos* found the advantages of a conjoined culture and they tried to demonstrate its qualities as much to the natives as to their own families. They managed to do so: both groups ended by accepting them. As years passed this generation managed to transform the new into the traditional and I, like others born to these innovators, was born already *gaucha-judía*.

There was one aspect of identity, though, in which my grandmother did not allow her daughters to differentiate themselves or distinguish themselves from her. Having been born female, they were weak like she, and they had to think, feel and act as such. After all was said and done, from her weakness my grandmother had gotten almost everything she'd desired, and she believed that weakness defined and would always define women.

In my grandparents' time, the strong—always male—enjoyed privileges that inhered in his position. He needed the best piece of meat so that he could stay in good shape for working; at siesta time, when he was regrouping, one had to maintain a sacrosanct silence; sex as a ritual to relieve tension, for which the wife in her role as hole had to be always available, was an obligation. But the strong also had to assume certain responsibilities: to work in order to acquire shelter and nourishment for himself and his family; to confront dangers alone, without letting them bother the family; to keep his fears and insecurities to himself, because his wife was not prepared to bear life's difficulties.

The weak,—always female-, enjoyed in turn the privileges of her condition: to enjoy life's little domestic pleasures without worrying about what went on outside; not to worry about the burden of providing for her family; not to have to make decisions and so not to risk making a wrong decision; not to take responsibility for herself or for her family's future. But the weak also paid the dues of her condition: she could not choose how to dispose of her body, as her sexuality did not belong to her; she could not satisfy her own desires, be they what they might, as she lacked economic, emotional, and social resources; she did not feel herself to be a person in her own right.

My grandmother longed for her daughters to have successful lives from their weak positions. She wanted them to know how to live by their wits, as survivors of oppression know how to do, and she wanted them to comport themselves correctly in their proper roles as wives, mothers, housewives.

Like my grandmother, my grandfather believed in doing what he had to do. He took on the responsibility of protecting his family and of providing them with the best life he could. To fulfill his responsibilities, he made all the decisions himself, making sure not to worry my grandmother with problems she couldn't manage. Both recognized themselves as victims of persecutions: first, pogroms in Russia; later, droughts, famines and difficulties in adapting to their new land. My grandmother worried about my grandfather's rigidity and limited horizons, but she never questioned his orders because she felt protected by them. If one was intolerable to her or went against her wishes, she could always pretend not to have heard, not to have understood, or she could disobey in secret. And so José always felt respected as the head of the family. Such was marital happiness at the time.

My grandmother thought that her husband, owner of all decisions and of the resources that made possible the fulfillment of his desires, presented a potential danger. As the strong one, he could harm her and her children. By contrast, as someone without the decision-making power and without her own life— that's to say, as a weak woman—she saw herself as unable to harm anyone else. She never imagined that her daughters' romantic difficulties could have anything to do with her way of requiring from them a dedication bordering on self-sacrifice.

When Elisa, the woman who would become my mother was born, Rosa cried, not knowing what to do with this newborn, in a far-off land, with a strange language and strange customs, without her mother's help or even the sister with whom she had emigrated, who'd also married a man she barely knew. Rosa still suffered from mother-hunger when she became a mother for the first time. Elisa became a mother when she breathed her first breath; she was born to end Rosa's solitude, to fill the void that existed within her, to warm her with her tender little body. I imagine that my future mother had barely entered the world when she knew that her destiny was to care for, protect, embrace, and feed all those who looked to her with mother-hunger.

Elisa dedicated herself to caring for others: she was her mother's nurse, her siblings' mother, her father's cook, and a symbol of home for everyone. She never let anyone know that she had rejected a marriage offer from a good prospect because she didn't feel she had the right to her own family. According to the way of loving she had learned from her mother—and from her father—she belonged to whomever needed her.

Everyone considered her an avowed old maid when she received a letter from the man who loved her, who kept loving her despite her rejection of him. From a house a few blocks away from hers, Marcos wrote to her:

"Charata, 3 September 1930

Dear Elisa:

Regarding your ideas about love, permit me to disagree. There are in everyone two distinct beings, two different kingdoms, as the Bible says, struggling with one another. They are not cleanly separated; instead, at times they become confused and produce a hybrid that is neither good nor bad. This new being, composed of two parts, can barely speak for itself, and as it possesses the characteristics of both the one and the other without having either one perfectly defined, it can with difficulty make itself understood. I don't know if you understand what I mean.

It is precisely this spiritual indecision that provokes the most suffering.

We do not always explain to ourselves what we are feeling and the result of this is a constant battle that ends by consuming body and soul.

Men are good, Elisa, and I don't doubt that a woman like you is capable of doing what both he and you find necessary in married life. Don't let yourself be carried away by pessimism. You are free, free, utterly free to make your decision and to be happy.

Your friend who wishes to be good,

Marcos"

My aunts, her sisters, said that Elisa didn't marry Marcos because she didn't love him enough. My uncles, her brothers, thought that Marcos didn't know how to fight for her and how to break her dependence on her family. I prefer the explanation given by the wife of one of my uncles, the only person in my family who denounced my grandmother's manipulations: My aunt Clara thought that Rosa was not only weak but also selfish. She was more interested in satisfying her own desires than was José who, although as the strong one he disposed of all the resources to which she had access, nevertheless used them for the good of the whole family. According to Clara, José was a little dumb and very easy to manipulate.

My mother, used to giving and caring without asking for anything in return, did not even consider the possibility of changing her position in life. Marcos offered her his nurture, he respected her emotions and her ideas, he encouraged her to think of herself, in addition to thinking of others. Marcos was readier to give than to ask for love. Elisa rejected him.

Instead, my mother accepted Luis, who demanded that she calm his demons and pardon his mistreatment of her. As convincing as Rosa in his demands for care, Luis was even better at manipulating Rosa with pain and guilt. On April 24, 1934, shortly before marrying and seven years before I was born, from the same village in northern Argentina, during a night that exuded a heavy and deafening silence—the dust had piled up for months without any rains, locusts were devouring the cotton that had not yet been harvested—my future father wrote:

> "Elisa, my soul:
> Since I left your house I've been very sad, neurasthenic. I feel a very suffocating oppression. I'm scared. I need you to smile at me with that smile that makes me forget everything, but I cannot ask you to do so. I am suffering so much that even knowing that these words will cause you pain I can't stop myself from writing them. Forgive me, my Elisa. They are things so intimate, thoughts so hidden, that I'm ashamed to even think them. One day you'll know. Can you understand even a little

the martyrdom of feeling that you've got powerful wings which are unable to flap? Write to me, calm me, and forgive me for this and for that which you might suffer in the future. Make these strange and tormenting thoughts leave me.

Luis"

Luis did not seem to love her but he showed her how much he needed her. He was able to capture her from the maternal embrace without helping her to liberate herself: to satisfy her mother's demands meant to entrap herself in his networks of emotional demands. My mother married a man who surpassed my grandmother in neediness at a time when the categories of strong and weak no longer served to define men and women. According to the trends of that time, people were supposed to choose freely who and how they wanted to be. Progress had come to the world of feelings and modernity demanded that everyone act as a subject of his own story, making vital decisions based on his own convictions. Everyone was supposed to be responsible for himself, choosing between the good and the bad, between acting rightly or wrongly.

My mother and my father learned from their parents that women were weak and men, strong. From their peers, they learned that women as well as men could and had to choose between being good and being bad.

In my grandparents' time, the adjectives strong and weak, as descriptors of qualities inherent in the sexes, seemed unchanging. In my parents' time, good and bad were acquired characteristics, personal decisions made by men and women. These concepts, which determined my parents' and grandparents' sentimental choices, did not establish religious or moral courts, they neither judged nor sent anyone to heaven or hell. They referred to the implementation of personal desires. To be good was to do what the other wanted and to be bad was to do what you yourself wanted.

The ideological criteria that determined my parents' romantic destiny, and in turn my own, stated that to be good was to be generous, altruistic, self-abnegating, resigned and ready to suffer on someone else's behalf. To be bad, by contrast, meant to be selfish, narcissistic, incapable of sacrifice for the good of others, and ready to use all available resources (including those of those who loved you) for your own ends.

To be good is to have feelings in relation to others, to connect emotionally with others. The highest expression of this quality is the ability to sacrifice, to give up everything (including one's own life, if necessary) for love of the other. The highest desire of someone good is to make the other happy by satisfying all his needs.

To be bad is to be unmoved, not to be carried away by one's emotions, to cut all sentimental ties, if necessary, in order to meet one's own needs and not to suffer. The highest expression of this quality is to show a total lack of sentiment, an absolute control over oneself, so that the needs and desires of the other are unable to interfere with one's own needs and desires.

"Your friend who wishes to be good," Marcos had written to express his desire to make my mother happy; he believed that to do what she wished would also make him happy. My father, by contrast, considered himself bad: he knew that he abused my mother's nurture of and care for him in order to satisfy his sexual and emotional desires, and he wondered why he wasn't happy, since he was doing what he wanted without thinking about what she wanted.

If the strong is he who has the resources to obtain and then to defend what he wants, and the bad is he who does as he likes; if the weak is he who lacks the resources to obtain or to defend what he wants and the good is he who does what the other wants, the conclusion seems almost comically preordained: the strong are bad, since they can do as they like and the weak are good, since they can only do what the other wants. Infused from childhood with these emotional textures, I always wondered who was the happier: the bad or the good, the strong or the weak? The stupid or the smart? He who sees and knows or he who neither sees nor knows, nor wishes to know?

Some women of my mother's generation chose only to be weak as their mothers had been: they used survivors' strategies and they felt themselves wholly innocent. Some men of my father's generation chose only to be strong as their fathers had been: they felt themselves wholly justified in enjoying the privileges that accrued, until their time, to the sex considered superior.

Other women, like my mother, and other men, like my father, found themselves trapped between two paradigms: the traditional one of the weak woman and the strong man and the modern one that mandated to both the responsibility of being either bad or good. These people succumbed to the conflict and remained emotionally divided for their whole lives. Men like my father suffered because they felt that they were bad without knowing how to be good; women like my mother suffered because they felt that they were weak without being able to be strong.

If my mother had been only weak, she might have married Marcos and gotten everything she wanted from him through manipulation. But acting like Rosa—whom she loved and whose subordination to her father pained her—had made her feel that she would be bad to selfishly let herself be cared for by a good husband. Unlike my grandmother, who never saw herself as responsible for her own decisions and who never evaluated her emotional attitudes from an ethical point of view, my mother questioned her own decisions and emotions from a very young age. She never made others responsible for her problems or difficulties. Exaggerating her ethical rigor, she often accepted as her own blame that which should have been borne by others.

On April 25, 1934, Elisa answered her future husband:

"Luis:
You were right to say that your letter would hurt me. I've read it so many times but I still don't understand it. What hurts the most is that if I can't understand you, I can't make you feel better. You have to admit that you're very mysterious in not saying the reason for your suffering. I don't know to what your sentence about "having

powerful wings that you can't flap" refers. I recognize that I am totally useless with metaphors. Do you think I suffer less if I don't understand your preoccupations?

It makes me very ashamed to be unable to interpret what you are saying. Perhaps it's because I've cultivated my own way of being and my own soul so much that I am unable to understand another's way of being.

I don't know of what I am supposed to pardon you. I don't feel offended about anything. The guilty party is me because maybe it's my fault that what is happening to you is happening. Please tell me, because if not we'll be following the wrong path. There should not be anything hidden between us. We should get to know each other now and not be taken by surprise later.

I hope that you think of the beauty of our affection and that you calm down.

Your soul kisses you with all her strength.

Elisa."

My father's strange and tormented ideas never left him. Both my parents suffered through forty years of marriage. When she was widowed, my mother re-took her father's surname: she decided to abandon forever her identity as a married woman together with the surname of her bad husband.

In accordance with the moral customs of the time when these letters were written, husbands were supposed to keep their badness in a socially bounded space. Passion and affection, body and soul, being in love with and loving circulated in different social territories in my parents' world. My father found the hypocrisy of this divided world—that which forced men to expend excess sexual energy away from home, to protect women from the low instincts that men hid in order to be strong—disagreeable, but he was not prepared to give up the advantages of this disassociation. He felt badly about not loving his wife with passion, for not seeing her as someone sensual and capable of being impassioned, but neither did he want a woman with these characteristics as the mother of his children. He wanted to think of himself as good, to think of her generously. But how could he do that without running the risk that she might choose a complete love, rather than a love broken into pieces?

My mother's eyes opened onto the soul; they reflected the candor of her hopes and the honesty of her acceptance. Her gaze transmitted the certainty of someone who trusts in communication. She was good and she believed in love. But she lacked the resources to defend her beliefs at home and being weak made her angry. Being angry made her feel that she was bad. Thus, she didn't know whether she was good or bad.

My father's eyes opened onto the body; they reflected the mistrust in his heart, the fear of imminent danger. His gaze transmitted the skepticism of someone who expected miscommunication. He was strong and he believed in power. But he was not happy imposing his beliefs on others at home and he felt guilty for being bad. Feeling guilty made him feel weak. Thus, he didn't know whether he was strong or weak.

The sons and daughters of people like my parents, difficult to fit into fixed emotional categories, inherited the parents' emotional uncertainties.

2

CROSSED EMBRACES

In the amorous miss-encounter that produced me, I grew up wondering every day which parent I should imitate: should I be like my father or like my mother?

The memory of my father teaching my brother and me the choreography of boxing, as the plants on the terrace sweated off the morning dew of the torrid mornings of my childhood, is as compelling as the memory of my mother in the kitchen of that same house, hours later, showing us how to cook for an extended family. To destroy or to heal, to make disappear or to make grow, to think or to feel, to dissent or to consent, to be strong or to be good, opposing apprenticeships that determined my way of being.

In my intimate feelings, even today it's hard for me to recognize myself as the daughter of both my mother and my father; it's hard to identify myself, at the same time and with the same intensity, with the best of each of them. Even today I feel that I abandon my mother if, in imitating my father, I am stronger than she; even today I feel that I betray my father if, in imitating my mother, I am better than he. Even today I am scared to be left alone—without any embrace at all—if I decide not to model myself completely on anyone, if I accept my strange, ambiguous, sometimes confused mixture of the identities of both. Even today I don't know how to lessen my anguish when I need maps in order to understand and be understood by my loved ones, and the idea of losing myself on the far side of the coordinates that oriented my parents' lives terrifies me. I am already at the age of a grandmother; my parents have been dead for many years. And still, the contradictory wills and desires of my parents jostle within me without reaching an easy or permanent harmony. For my brother, it is the same.

He and I, like so many others of our generation, learned how to live in two different emotional worlds: that of men, where our fathers lived, and that of women, where our mothers lived. There were no gray zones in the bifurcated universe in which we grew up.

The fathers-men-powerful ones reigned in the world of work that existed away from home. The domestic world existed inside the home and there reigned our mothers-women-loving ones.

The ways of thinking and feeling were different in each part, in each territory, in each sex. Neither respected the ways of the other but they acted as if they were mutually necessary, mutually imperative. The oppositions related to one another through confrontation: they seemed to complete one another through complementarity.

The childhood gazes of some men and women of my generation caught the unspoken curiosity and the envy, often transmuted into scorn, with which our fathers and mothers perceived each other. We intuited that our fathers, supposedly emotionally illiterate, longed for the unconditional affection that children in those days gave only to their mothers; we guessed that our mothers, supposedly professionally illiterate, longed for the respect of their opinions and ideas that children in those days gave only to their fathers.

Women like myself learned to feel attracted by the vertiginous sounds of liberty, passion and mystery that came from outside. We were not content to listen to them from afar, as we knew would happen if we lived as our mothers had, entrapped by domestic tasks. The consuming force and the mysterious pull of our fathers' world fascinated us.

Men like my brother learned to feel attracted by the intimate whispers and scents of tenderness that reached them from inside.

They were not content to see them from afar as they knew would happen if they lived as their fathers had, entrapped by the need to make money while battling against professional enemies. The nurturing protection and calming familiarity of their mothers' world fascinated them.

We knew that each of our parents had great scorn for their need of the other: our fathers, for needing their wives in order to attain family belonging and family love; our mothers, for needing their husbands in order to attain social standing and social power. We knew (our parents made sure that we knew) that each wanted to free himself from the other. Convinced that the only route to liberty (for our fathers, emotional; for our mothers, economic) consisted of making themselves have the other's skills, some mothers and fathers encouraged in their vassals a desire to be like the other, to be the other.

They treated our brothers as if they wanted them, despite their being men, to be good, a quality then used almost synonymously with feminine; and they treated us as if they wanted us, despite our being women, to be strong, a quality then used almost synonymously with masculine. Our mothers could not be strong nor our fathers good; but our mothers sowed in their daughters and our fathers sowed in their sons the seeds of the desire to learn how to live as the inhabitants of the other world lived.

Some mothers and fathers were active participants in the attraction of their opposite-sex children towards their own territories, their own ways of living, their own forms of thinking and feeling. And so some women and men of my generation learned rapidly and efficiently how to speak the language of our opposite-sex parent.

Elisa, my mother, urged me to abandon her way of life and to learn that of my father: "You have to be self-sufficient so you can pick the husband you want. You shouldn't feel obligated to stay in a marriage simply because you can't feed yourself or your children." Many women of my mother's generation, like her, pushed their daughters out from the domestic jail. She wanted me to be freer than she: that is, to be stronger. I wanted to avenge the dignity that had been undermined by my father's affairs, but I feared being contaminated by her weakness and being unable to enjoy, as my father did, the liberty of movement that would allow me to satisfy my personal desires, without asking for permission.

At the same time, my mother insisted that I be as good as she, because that was how women were and would always be. When all was said and done, from her bondage she had managed to be very loved—more than her husband—by her children, her family, and anyone else she cared for. It's true: she never found a man to love her passionately but neither had she been very interested in this kind of love. Being a mother had been so important that she was a mother even to her husband. She wanted merely that her daughters choose more wisely than she had the men with whom we would be good.

Because I was only a woman, my father didn't fear me as a future competitor and he allowed me to learn all his battle secrets, a generosity that was not apparent in his relationship with my brother. My mother didn't want me to be as weak as she and so her embrace was one that pushed me away, that distanced me from her feminine territory. No one realized that this way of encouraging me to be stronger than her would distance me as well from her way of being good.

At the same time, my father, Luis, embroiled my brother in other contradictions. "What makes a man worthwhile is his sensibility, his ability to be moved, to feel, to savor words." My father's words, if not his actions, taught my brother that another life was possible. And so my brother also obeyed a migratory mandate: he didn't want to live in a constant state of war, didn't want to act as if he had natural rights over his partner, didn't want to exercise power through constant competition with other men. He preferred to love a woman whom he also admired, just as earlier he had entered into our mother's domestic world and questioned our father's manner of fulfilling the role of head of the family.

Unlike me, my brother didn't need to confront my mother as I did in my desire to differentiate myself from her, and so he was able to learn all of her skills in tenderness and sensibility. No one realized that this way of not being as bad as my father would also distance my brother from my father's way of being strong.

Our fathers' world was ruled by the love of power, our mothers', by the power of love. The rules that organized the public sphere were exactly the opposites of those that organized the private sphere. The abilities needed to triumph in each world were mutually exclusive. The systems of reward and punishment were so antagonistic that a gain in one world was a loss in the other and vice-versa.

Some women and men of my generation learned that in the world of love you won by loving more, by being more generous, by giving more, by ingratiating oneself more. You won by extending the limits of your individuality so much that you forgot yourself, lost yourself in the other, fused yourself to the other in an idyllic embrace. The magic formula was: "the other is more important than me; I win by loving him and disappearing into him." The almost religious epiphany that arose from feeling oneself flooded by one's bond to and gratitude for the other was the culmination of this romantic path, and its key phrase was *to give*.

Our mothers taught us, by their example, that emotional self-esteem was measured by degrees of generosity, of giving oneself completely, of pleasing the other to the point of self-sacrifice. In the community of the domestic world, passive resignation formed part of the path towards a successful bond. Some of our mothers pushed themselves to be good as gold, to be the best. They never suspected that this kind of bond could enslave men and alienate them, make them feel almost pariahs without any rights, by excluding them from the world of tender and domestic love in which our mothers reigned.

In the world of power, you won by being loved, by acquiring more and ending up with the most offers, by getting the best piece. You won by making sure that your ego defined the collective *we,* by extending the limits of your individuality so that you forgot the other and made him into an appendage, by making your colleagues want to fuse with you and disappear. The magic formula was: "I'm more important than the other; I win if he loves me and subordinates himself to me." The feeling of triumph over others" wills, consumed to the point of total subordination, was the culmination of this romantic path, and its key phrase was *to take.*

Our fathers taught us, by example, that emotional self-esteem was measured in degrees of egoism, of being able to fulfill one's own desires utterly, extraditing the other in order to do so. To be hard, aggressive, conquering formed part of the abilities required to conquer what was yours every day. In the work world, active arrogance was part of being competent, of the path towards the triumph of power. Some of our fathers pushed themselves to be stronger than strong, to be the strongest. They never suspected that strength could be a way of enslaving women and of alienating them, of making them feel almost like pariahs without any rights, in the world of passion and force in which our fathers reigned.

In the world of love one needed the patience of a farmer. One had to know how to be, how to wait, how to attend to and trust the processes of growth. The cyclical time of the harvest, ritualistic and repetitive, rooted one into this world.

In the world of power one needed the agility of the hunter. One had to know how to move, how to search for the best opportunity, how to stay alert to every possible movement of one's prey. The open, flexible time of the hunter made one into a nomad.

In the world of love one's admiration of the other marked out the path to be followed: keeping him at whatever cost was how one won. In the world of power one's scorn for the other marked out the path: eliminating him at whatever cost was how one won.

In the world of love one was sustained by tenderness and moral conventions; social traditions, and responsibility to the proper forms were respected. In the world of power one was sustained by passion and originality; creativity and immediate necessities were respected.

Some women and men of my generation wanted to cross emotional frontiers in order to improve our lives and broaden our horizons. We women wanted to define ourselves as whole people, as complete human beings. We wanted to live in the public sphere of money and professional satisfaction. The world of power fascinated us and seemed exotic, so different from the domestic world with which we were so familiar and which bored us to tears, too tranquil as presented by our weak and dependent mothers. Our brothers wanted access to the world of intimacy and sensibility. For them, the world of love was fascinating and exotic, different from the known dangers of the exciting but excessive hunts into which their fathers, bad and authoritarian, pushed them.

We learned in a criss-crossed way, my brother and me. I learned the rules of the game of power before knowing the dictionary's definition of the word as: "capacity, strength, the potential to do, to authorize, to order, and to dispose of or to someone or something." I learned to be strong, almost a pugilist against life. My brother learned the rules of the game of love— "the sentiment that extends towards something or someone and the attitude of care and benevolence towards others"—and so he was good, as good as bread, as we say in Argentina. Even today he shows his emotions more spontaneously and more directly than I do and his crimping of the borders of the Jewish-*gaucha empanada* is better than my own. Even today my attacks are more effective, more substantial than his and I'm firmer than he in my decisions. Both of us learned to speak the language of the world we migrated to. These criss-crossed apprenticeships transformed us into people both more complete and more complex than our parents. My brother learned how to feel and I, to think.

The migratory process from the private to the public sphere was long and difficult for some women of my generation, as many of our stories make clear.

We had to suffer attacks from women of our generation who clung to domestic traditions, defending with claws and teeth the old ways of being female. They refused to leave the sacred precincts of home and hearth, vindicated the advantages of the "feminine" emotions and of the perfection of the subtleties and intricacies of the language of love. They accused us of abandoning and betraying them, of behaving like men.

We also suffered attacks from men of our generation who defended with claws and teeth the old ways of being male. They refused to let us gain access to economic privilege, insisted upon the difficulties we would have in understanding the complexity of sophisticated "male" thoughts, told us we would never master the vocabulary of the language of power. We would always be women.

We didn't fit into the housewife group. But neither did we fit into the businessman group. We did not fit in, we did not have a name, we did not exist. We felt accused of being too masculine, of pretending to work like men, as much as we felt accused of being too feminine when we allowed our emotions to interfere with our professional lives. We ourselves felt that we were not feminine enough: that we devoted too little time to our appearance, to taking care of our husbands and children, of taking care of the little details of daily life. But we also felt that we were not masculine enough: we could not give orders, nor demand anything of anyone else, nor fight nor defend ourselves without crying. Our desires for a complete life had taken us down a path on which many times we felt half-people, part-people, bifurcated, people broken in two.

Some women tolerated neither the ambiguities suffered during the process of migration nor the difficult contradictions between feelings and thoughts nor the complexities of emotional and intellectual paradoxes. These women preferred to adopt entirely "masculine" ways of working; they appropriated power and all its attributes, they chose to be professional, to be dry. They assimilated completely into the new way of being. They stopped being housewives and they refused to define themselves as mothers or wives. They changed their habits, clothing, mentality, ways of feeling. To defend themselves against attacks from their male colleagues, they renounced their feminine pasts and forgot the feminine knowledge learned from their mothers.

But, just as the *gaucha-judía* way of being proved to be enriching and satisfying for my mother and some of her peers, so some of my generational peers managed to break the dichotomy: we created a complex professional identity. Our way of being *women-professionals* inaugurated an unlooked-for and happy reconstruction of the world of the professional sentiments: we knew how to be strong like our fathers and good like our mothers, at the same time and with the same intensity.

And we could practice this new way of being thanks to men who, like my brother, began to be as good as our mothers while remaining as strong as our fathers: they accepted us into their professional terrains.

In the sixties, professional men and recently professional women did not know one another; we scared each other and we mistrusted each other. To overcome our lack of identity and to create a new way of being, feeling and thinking, both they and we had to learn how to discriminate, how to discern. We had to learn how to decode, how to translate each other, to understand when they were right to criticize us for letting ourselves be carried away by "feminine" emotions and when they were wrong not to learn from us, to treat these emotions as a fundamental source of information about intuitive forms of thought of which they were ignorant. For our part, we had to recognize when they were stubbornly refusing to share power, and when they were, by contrast, simply pointing out that an idea of ours was wrong. They and we had to learn when and how to confide in the other, when to protect ourselves from him. When and how to speak in which language, that of power or that of love. When and how to recognize that we did not understand the other's language, when and how to ask what they meant, which required that we women overcome our fear of being attacked by them and that they overcome their fear of being rejected by us.

Some men learned that, sometimes, we said "I feel" when we meant to say "I think." They learned how to value our ways, apparently disorganized, of taking care of various things at once.

They observed our ways of introducing subjective information into objective decision-making and learned how to decide when such introductions did or did not work. And we learned from them how to incorporate concepts such as justice into subjective decision-making. Together we created a new shared language, a code that allowed us to translate each other, understand each other, and enrich each other in the professional terrain.

Some women defended the bastion of the world of power; others defended completely the world of love. But a third group developed an alternative vision: we didn't want to assimilate completely the lifestyle that the masculine professional culture taught us but, at the same time, we rejected the idea of being entrapped in the feminine domestic culture. We thought, felt, and acted in a way different from that of women who defined themselves as housewives as well as from that of men who defined themselves as professionals. And we came in time to have a name, to constitute an accepted and legitimate feminine way of being, as *women-professionals*.

Today I know that I am not "odd" because I work: I do not abandon my mother when I earn money using some of the emotional resources she gave me from her housewife position; neither do I betray my father when I manage to be more loved than he by using some of the intellectual resources he gave me from his professional life.

When people speak of my smile, of my gaze, of the calm or peacefulness I transmit, I know that they speak of my mother. I recognize her *curandera* presence in each of my gestures as a therapist. In the imaginary code of arms with which I represent myself professionally, a cooking pot takes center stage. My mother, already dead but more alive than ever in me, urges me to nurture sincerely, cleanly, healthfully, and sometimes exaggeratedly, anyone who asks for such care. I transform her kitchen recipes into conceptual ones, using a vocabulary I learned first from my father and then from my professional training. And when people speak of my intellectual enthusiasm, I recognize my father's sometimes dogmatic passion. Already dead but more alive than ever in me, he urges me to defend my ideas ardently, with a bravery at times overly stubborn.

I have inherited both ways of being in my way of being a *woman-professional*. I see myself as equally my mother's daughter as my father's: from her, I've inherited wisdom and common sense; from him, intelligence and intellectual curiosity. For years I mistakenly acted as if Athena were the daughter of Zeus alone, as if my professional competency came only from what I'd gained from my father. But over the years I've remembered that the warrior goddess of intelligence gestated in the womb of Metis, Wisdom, and that there she was nurtured until her powerful father, threatened by her mother's profound and soulful way of understanding the world, swallowed up both mother and daughter in order to give birth himself.

Sometimes I think that I've only formalized or legalized my mother's intuitive way of working. Friends, neighbors and relatives consulted her all the time for help with their doubts, anxieties and problems. They asked her to cure their deafness by removing ear wax, a skill she had learned from the Indians of Chaco, whose children, in turn, I taught how to write; they asked her to provide counsel and guidance to young women about their emotional futures, to young men about their professional ones; they asked her to provide a new context for their worries, a glimpse of the future results of a test, a business deal, or a voyage. Although people consult me over other matters and although I receive money as well as gratitude for my advice, my ways of being in the world and in time, like my sources of happiness and of worry, resemble those of my mother. I know too that I've written this book and wrote others because my father gave me his curiosity for the written word, that I speak English because my father urged me to continue my studies, that big cities don't scare me, as Buenos Aires did when I was young and unprotected by the rural ways of my mother, because he taught me to love traveling.

I wanted to inhabit both my mother's world of love and my father's world of power at the same time. I wanted to be good and strong at the same time and, in my professional life, I was able to do so.

But it was much harder and more painful, and I made many more mistakes and hurt many more people, in the process of trying to reconcile my desire to be loved tenderly, inherited from my mother, with my desire to be respected passionately, inherited from my father.

My way of inhabiting the familiar territory was not complex but confused; not ample but ambiguous; not paradoxical but contradictory. In the world of love, my way of being didn't include self-abnegation, the resigned and excessive bonding of my mother's loving embrace. My embrace, like that of many women of my generation, consisted of the hand-to hand combat of two sets of individuals, as we'd learned from our fathers. We knew that we were stronger than our mothers but we also believed that we were not as good as they.

It was also confusing, ambiguous, and contradictory to inhabit the professional sphere as my brother did. In the world of power, men such as he felt weak; their styles of argumentation didn't go over well with the violent, decided, provocative force of the powerful embraces of men like my father. Habituès of the tender, merging embrace of their mothers, they didn't strike unwomanly women like myself as men with whom to fall in love.

At home, women like me and men like my brother did not know how to conjoin the languages of love and power.

We knew that we were destined to two embraces: we women, the embrace we scorned, from our mothers, and the one we feared, from our fathers; men like my brother, the embrace they rejected, from their fathers, and that they idealized, from their mothers. We were no one and nothing, emotionally: not masculine men, not masculinized women, not feminine women, not effeminate men. We scorned and feared ourselves, we rejected and idealized ourselves, at the same time and with the same intensity.

Meanwhile, those fathers and mothers who had pushed us towards the territories of our opposite-sex parents now made us feel like strangers in the worlds of our same-sex parents. Our mothers said, of us, "she's *your* daughter," when they feared that we had differentiated ourselves too much and had become too strong. Our fathers said of our brothers, too different and hence too good, "he's *your* son."

None of us—neither the women nor the men of my generation—knew how to dance the dances of a romantic couple. We sometimes paid a bit of attention to our incompetency, but we could not tolerate the untruth of our favorite statement: where there's a will there's a way. We refused to truly own up to our mistakes, and we perpetuated them in the emotional memories of our daughters and sons.

3

LIBERAL LOVES

Every time I recount my romantic history, I remember some verses that Chico Buarque wrote, based on a Brazilian children's song. In his version he says:

> *"O primeiro me chegou como quem vem do florista,*
> *trouxe um bicho de pelucia, trouxe um broche de amatista.*
> *Me contou suas viagens, e as vantagens que ele tinha,*
> *me mostrou o seu relogio, me chamava de rainha.*
> *Me encontrou tão desarmada que tocou meu coração,*
> *mais não me negava nada e assustada eu disse não."*

(The first one came to me as if from the florist's
with a stuffed animal, with an amethyst brooch.
He spoke of his voyages, of the advantages he'd had,
He showed me his watch, he called me his queen.
He found me so unarmed that he touched my heart,
But he refused me nothing and, scared, I said no.)

My first suitor offered to share the world of power with me. Mario was five years older than me and very suave, he'd gone to good bilingual schools. He was sporty and hardworking and showed promise in the business world. Without doubt, a good match.

At the start of the sixties, I hadn't finished my studies and the money I made barely paid for the psychoanalytic sessions that were so necessary for my professional training. I was barely making ends meet. To let myself be taken care of by a strong man who acted like he believed in me seemed to be a vital and unique opportunity. He would refuse me nothing, as long as I never opened the door of the golden cage he proffered as a house, of which he held the only key.

Mario encouraged me to keep studying and he celebrated my good grades as long as the books didn't keep me away from the hairdresser's or from being impeccably dressed to meet his foreign friends. My job was to take care of him; my free time was filled by his needs. Of course he wanted me to learn languages, to go to modern dance classes, to dabble in art. Mario wanted a complete woman at his side. A good housewife, a sexually mature woman, an intellectual companion. What more did I want? I could do whatever I wanted, as long as I accepted the role of wife.

I had to cede all agency to him, to control my imperious need of showing my own strength. I could do so only obliquely, demanding of him more economic triumphs, comparing him to more powerful men, scorning him if he didn't seem sufficiently strong. I was to help him improve his standing in the competitive masculine jungle by communicating my criticisms coyly, without confronting him.

He offered me the role of a great woman behind the success of a future great man. Publicly I had to play my assigned role as the weak one, but privately we both knew that I was also strong— not only as a mother, as had been the case for my mothers' generation, but also as a wife. Mario thought of himself as good and thought that his model of partnership was democratic and egalitarian. He needed me by his side and he needed me to appear to come from his side in the world of men: my presence as a professional woman, as agile with the head as with the heart, would strengthen his position as a strong man. If he attained a relationship with a woman like that, it would prove that not only was he powerful, but he was also intelligent. His only condition was that I put my intelligence at his service, under his direction, in the conjugal project. If I followed his orders, together we would be the best and we would win in the world of power.

He asked me to take responsibility for his social life and social advancement, that I use my knowledge of psychology to help him to develop effective strategies to use in his work life. He honored my abilities as a social seductress as long as I used them in the service of his business activities, helping him to create a good image. It wasn't a bad deal, as my salary depended on my merits: the better the publicity I generated for him, the more I helped secure him a good position in the competitive masculine market, the better it would be for both of us.

The double game of giving and taking made me his passionate admirer, the most loyal spectator of his social advances, a demanding critic who had to be won over. As an enemy to be conquered—my intimate role—I made him feel powerful thanks to his seduction of a hard-to-catch prey; he used this potency for new social, professional and public conquests. My job in his personal business would be to make him feel the pleasure of winning me over, to disguise myself as bad in order to introduce a *frisson* of erotic danger into our relationship. But I could only play this game when he asked me to, and otherwise I had to confirm his sense of me as weak, dependent, domesticated.

It was a relationship like my grandmother's. I was authorized to have whims, to manipulate him to get what I wanted. That would be a secret demonstration of my dependency. His generosity ratified his strength, my humility guaranteed my loyalty.

Scared, I said no.

Scared, really, less of him than of myself.

I feared finding myself full of savage and uncontrolled impulses if I gave free rein to myself. I feared being too unfeminine if I showed all my force. I feared not knowing how to pretend and how to behave hypocritically like a proper little thing. I knew that I was not good at the only defensive resource permitted to the woman-who-hides-her-strength-in-order-to-marry-a-strong-man: emotional manipulations. My mother, too honest and demanding of herself, had refused to learn these techniques which her mother used without remorse; for my part, I was too enraged at my grandmother, who robbed me of my mother's attention, to think for a minute of imitating her.

I feared being unable to play the game Mario proposed and to end by losing: to do what he wanted thinking that I was doing what I wanted. I didn't feel good enough to win using the rules of the game of love (obeying and satisfying all his desires) nor strong enough to win using the rules of the game of power (demanding that he respect my wishes.)

To make myself weak struck me as equally humiliating and false as to make myself good. I thought that both strategies accepted the enemy's terms, but neither took up the struggle for equality with men. Both strategies presupposed that the strong sex was the sole owner of social and economic power.

I didn't want to dance these choreographies of love. Mario and I didn't make a good couple. Our interests in life were incompatible. He wanted a woman I wasn't, I wanted a man he wasn't. He offered me a share in the celebrations of his victories in the world of power, I wanted the liberty to fight my own battles there. I wanted him to recognize my agency when I collaborated with him, he offered me recognition of such collaboration as if it were minor work, subordinate to the real task at hand. We were not playing in the same scene, we were neither compatible nor complementary. We each needed other partners in order to take the stage as we wished to do.

A few months after this discovery, I met Jorge, a man-who-wished-to-be-good, and he offered to share with me the world of love. His world. We met on a beach where we were both on vacation, both with recently broken-off engagements. We were barely in our twenties. The summer's magic enveloped us one night: we counted the stars with our kisses, as a popular song said.

I felt that I owned my desires, felt full of life, capable of directing my gaze towards new horizons and new people. I believed myself to be free and because of that freedom to choose

I explained to him that I neither accepted his love nor wanted to love him: "I've just regained my senses, I don't want to lose them again. I want to be myself," I remember telling him in a defiant tone.

A wise friend, who every so often gave me the gift of a sentence that put into words an indecipherable feeling, said to me: "Women look at men, men look at God. That's why men and women cannot regard one another properly. They do not see each other." At that moment, that summer, on that beach, I didn't want to look at God through the eyes of a man. I wanted to see him myself.

Jorge offered me the same unconditional love that my brother had learned from my mother. I didn't want to hurt him, to use him in the service of my desires. I worried that he was incapable of resisting me and I didn't want to be the stronger one. I feared myself.

Scared, I said no.

A strong man wasn't good for me because I felt that I was his victim. A good man wouldn't do either because I felt that I was his victor.

I had been entrapped between two emotional paradigms: the traditional, learned from my mother, that showed me the advantages of living as a good woman in the world of love; and the modern, learned from my father, that showed me the advantages of living as a strong woman in the world of power.

I didn't manage to emerge from my emotional nebulousness. I rejected the golden handcuffs in which a father-husband would imprison me, as I rejected the role of jailer of a brother-husband. I wanted to be free but not bad, to stretch my wings without destroying a man in my flight, as I felt my father had done to my mother. I knew I was strong and I wanted to meet someone good, but I feared that this meant giving up our original citizenships, transplanting our identities; I feared that the man would be the feminine and I the masculine element in the relationship. I was so confused that I preferred to be alone and I rejected Jorge just as my mother had rejected Marcos many years earlier.

A little while later, another man appeared in my life. Chico Buarque's song continues:

"*O segundo me chegou como quem chega do bar*
Trouxe um litro de aguardente tão amarga de tragar
Indagou o meu passado e cheirou minha comida
Vasculhou minha gaveta me chamava de perdida
Me encontrou tão desarmada que arranhou me coração
Mas não me entregava nada e assustada eu disse não."

(The second came to me as if from a bar
He brought a liter of bitter drink
He ravaged my past and tore through my food
He turned my drawers inside-out, he called me lost.
He found me so unarmed that he scratched my heart
But he gave me nothing and, scared, I said no.)

But in my case I said yes, I got married, and I lived with Omar, the father of my daughters, for twenty years.

During our first meeting he gave me a copy of *The Second Sex*. He had inscribed it as follows: "To love one another is not to gaze into each other's eyes but to look, together, at the world." Together with this key text in the history of contemporary feminine identity came the arrogant proposal that I recreate with him the relationship that Beauvoir had had with Jean-Paul Sartre. In a bold (and wrong-headed) act of omnipotence, I agreed.

"We are born alone and we die alone. Life is bitter, reality, hard. We are all each other's enemies. Every conscience seeks the death of the other," he said, paraphrasing Sartre paraphrasing Marx paraphrasing Hegel. Omar taught me a new dogma, existentialism as revealed truth.

According to these theories, I had fallen into the retrograde emotional webs of bourgeois relationships; waiting for me there was a lover who would take care of me like a parent forever if I didn't escape from the golden cage in which he was protecting (or trapping) me. By contrast, Omar offered me nothing less and nothing more than freedom. He didn't tempt me with promises of a home or a future. But he told me what he saw as the truth: "No one belongs to anyone. Love is a social lie designed to control and domesticate us. I will protect you from those who wish to entrap you. Be as intelligent as you can, go where you will. Take from the world what you wish."

This man, who played poker and bet on horses, who knew *The Iliad* by heart and sang George Brassens songs, who studied philosophy and earned his living driving a cab in the streets of Buenos Aires, explained that I wasn't bad for wanting to be strong. I was the victim of an oppressive cultural system. According to him, in rejecting Mario I had only defended my identity, even if I did not yet know of what that identity consisted.

He told me that with Mario I had played the role of princess, the favored but least important part of the patriarchy; it was right that I had rejected Mario. I should choose my own way of being. Omar encourage me to be a woman-person, although the person-Susana consumed the woman-Susana. For the first time in my life I felt that someone understood me, translated me, deciphered me. I was ready to pay any price to enjoy this emotion for as long as possible.

Omar opened the world's door to me, and he told me that we shouldn't waste time, in his words, looking at each other. He invited me to look with him at all humanity.

In gratitude for what he was teaching me, in the beginning of our time together, I gave Omar a little felt rabbit. He looked with disgust at the somewhat silly sign of my gratitude. "Don't you like it?" I asked, already knowing the answer. "No," he said, and to show how little he liked it, he threw it into the nearest trash can in a very *nouvelle vague* way. Omar didn't want to be good; he merely wished to be not too bad. His way of not being too bad was to insist that I was bad as well: in this way we would neutralize our mistreatment of one another, we would arm ourselves simultaneously, and neither would suffer. Such was his proposal.

I thought: "this man doesn't lie, he doesn't promise false love or love scenes. He doesn't try to buy me with loyalty. He tells me he's dangerous and that I shouldn't trust him. This is true freedom." If I was truly strong, I needed to be with someone who would not be destroyed by my desires for flight, for world-seeking.

He disappeared for days at a time to cure me of the vice of dependency, of security, of need to control his movements; in order not to let me give in to the temptation to abandon my search for freedom. The unexpected formed part of the everyday. He tried to make me feel that my life was in my own hands, not his; he was convinced of the truth of this. I could think that his erratic conduct left me abandoned or free, sad and alone or euphoric and in control. I could choose to decide which version of my emotions served me.

I preferred to think that we would liberate ourselves together. That together we would dance the steps of comradeship, of *free love*, of a joint rebellion against social hypocrisy. Love without complete liberty makes the lover vulnerable and the beloved weak: Omar taught me to repeat this mantra.

Our goal was to establish in our small way equality between men and women. Equality, for us, means the annihilation of differences. We defended an equality that sought to make men and women homologous. "To differentiate" sounded like "to discriminate" and discrimination was, for us, a bad word.

At the start, our dance was a party that both of us enjoyed. I quickly learned how to argue as he taught me; I was a young enthusiastic pupil who brought bodily energy to every immediate task. I gained the liberty to test myself in my flights over enemy territory, in the professional world of men, feeling myself held aloft and guided by one of them. For his part, Omar was a dedicated teacher, who opened the world of the mind and the heart of a dangerous, attractive man to me. Immersed in his own battle with the patriarchal world, he tried to destroy it using me, a woman who infiltrated that world. Helping me win he would also win the game of power; my successes were ours, were his. I shared them gratefully and I felt that I was a heroine of the emotional revolution.

Luis Sepúlveda, a contemporary poet, describes us thus:

> The women of my generation said:
> To everyone according to his necessity and his capacity
> for response
> As in battle blow for blow, in love kiss for kiss

And he continues:

> Because the women of my generation marked us
> With the indelible fire of their nails
> The universal truth of their rights . . .
> They respected only the limits that crossed borders,
> Internationalists in affection, love's brigadiers
> Commissars of *I love you*, militants of the caress

According to his words, we were "like a closed fist violently enclosing the world's tenderness." I recognize myself: in that time, women like me politicized love and fought for it.

Omar offered me a free relationship. He gave me—he thought he was giving me—the possibility to transform myself into a free and independent person. He didn't promise to protect me, or take care of me, or love me forever, or create with me a love nest.

One day, a few months after our first daughter, Natasha, was born, I called him at work and, enraged, told him that I'd figured it all out: he wanted to be my lover but not my husband. I didn't want the same and I thought that this conversation would make him understand. I was wrong. When he came home, late that night, he told me he'd gone out to celebrate with his friends my declaration of love. The best praise I could offer him was to recognize that he was not a husband, not one of those conventional despicable bureaucratic men.

I decided to enjoy what I could of this relationship with a man who didn't want to be a husband, and I dedicated myself to the perfection of my skills at inhabiting a masculine professional world. Omar convinced me that free love was the ideal dance for a couple. We believed that we had reached a romantic utopia and in so doing had entered history by changing what, until that time, had seemed the only possible model, the divided, rigid world of our ancestors.

I thought that if I concentrated on strengthening my personal desires and the tools for satisfying them, I would be happy.

I wasn't the only woman, nor was Omar the only man, who had decided that love between people was too small, too little. To raise it to the category of something sublime, something for which one might give one's life, meant dedicating love to a social cause. This decision seemed more important and transcendent that dedicating one's love to a single person.

Women and men of my generation chose this kind of love for various reasons. But the love relationship contained many common characteristics: it was more important to choose a companion than to look for a husband or a romantic encounter; it was old-fashioned to obey bourgeois romantic notions by suffering because of love for a man, waiting for his phone calls or tender gestures. One was supposed to dedicate oneself to progress: some of us focused on our careers, others, on artistic vocations, still others, on political activism. As long as our companions shared our ideas and walked with us on the same ideological path, we would be happy. Omar and I were happy—so I told myself.

Working gave me so much pleasure and so much gratification, in addition to money, that I didn't mind sharing everything with him. In this way I repaid him for leaving me free to do as I liked, for not requiring me to look after the house or attend to his emotional or sexual needs. He looked after himself, as men had to learn how to do to free themselves from women's domestic yoke, he told me. To each his own, this dance was called, this way of relating in which neither of us owed the other a thing: we didn't have to be at each other's beck and call nor make sacrifices for anyone's happiness but our own. We thought we had invented a new form of love, rebellious and controversial. We thought we had destroyed the barricades that separated our mothers from our fathers.

Men and women who wanted liberal partnerships lived together, literally—we lived *at the side of* the other, *next to* him or her, but not together *with* him or her.

Our progress let us travel in two worlds without needing mutual aid in constructing or reconstructing those worlds. We lived in the same house, we shared our children and our social and familial relationships, but each dealt with these things alone. Each member of the couple had the same rights and responsibilities, because we had to be equal: we had to both work outside and inside the home, to think and to feel in the same way, to be strong in the same way. We were so equal that we learned not to need one another for anything. We were together only because of our concurrent desires to be so. We loved each other freely, without any type of compromise.

Some women broke their financial dependency on men. We said no to the controlling security offered us by domestic prisons and learned how to support ourselves. But in liberating ourselves from men, we also liberated them from us.

At the start, they only abandoned their economic responsibilities. Soon they also abandoned their emotional responsibilities, thinking that, like us, they should be free to do as they liked. When we gave up our dependent position, we also gave up the manipulative power that weak women like my grandmother had used; we gave up the strength that made good women like my mother feel themselves the sole owners of the world of the emotions. We freed men from the moral obligation to take care of women and they as well as we forgot the emotional choreographies that our grandparents and parents, indeed all of our ancestors, had danced.

My second daughter, Paula, was born on March 8, International Women's Day. In that same year, 1974, the first feminist discussion group in Buenos Aires was also born, under my direction. My daughters, my friends, my home, my work, my women's group: I had all of that, then. More: I had myself, full, whole, rooted in myself. I didn't need a man to maintain me, to make me feel loved and valuable, or to calm my anguish. I had gotten out from under the bifurcated world of my grandparents and parents. Why not enjoy the world alone? Our daughters could enjoy two worlds, two houses, two families, two ways of living, each supposedly whole, each supposedly self-sufficient. In any case, as one of my daughters told me shortly after the separation, Omar was "almost a mother" and I was "almost a father." He would end up free of the burden of family and I of the burden of a man in my house. In that time began the trend of *live-out* husbands.

The expression came from the popular expressions for the two main forms of paid domestic work: there were live-in and live-out maids. The former slept in the houses where they worked and had no control over their own time. For their employers, the advantage was to be able to have constant help; the disadvantage was a loss of control, intimacy and privacy. Maids who lived out had their own lives but they didn't get what were considered the perks of housing and meals.

In each case, housewives and maids gained in some areas and lost in others. In the same way, women and men gained and lost in various ways depending on whether the husband lived in or out.

Omar and I thought that we both would gain a lot if he assumed definitively his role as lover and cast off that of husband, which he had never fully accepted anyway. We relied on information that would allow us to be allies or enemies: he showed me that I was a bad mother, I showed him he was a lazy worker. He showed me my adherence to the *people will say* of social opinion, which he described as feminine submission; I showed him his social ostracism, his inability to engage in dialogue, in which I saw masculine rigidity. Each strove to make his world of liberty better, to make it the best. There is no battle crueler or more violent than the one between equals, companions who intuit each other's every move and know each other from tip to toe.

TWO TO TANGO | 63

I thought that removing him from the domestic space and having a live-out husband would let me recover my agency within the home. I could recover my relationship with my daughters as well as my maternal power, both of which had been threatened by his suffocating and judging presence.

I woke up from the dream in July 1976.

In Argentina, the military government's repressions prevented the coming of "imagination to power" that had swept the world in May 1968. I also lost ground in my personal life: defeated, my imagination also went into hiding. The roof of my house literally fell in. I took this accident, despite its lack of major effects, as an alarm, a metaphor of my life situation.

Around those weeks, one of my best girlfriends had honored me with a toast: "For the final victory, I toast to you, the feminine Trotsky, from my place of Stalin". When I remembered that Trotsky had been killed in his Mexican exile by order, as some say, of his ex-comrade from the revolution, I felt scared. I saw in that toast an annunciation of the symbolic disappearance of the feminist Olympus that had been my emotional and ideological bulwark until that moment.

So ended, painfully, the first act of Liberal Loves. My relationship with Omar lasted almost fourteen years and ended when we realized that we were a woman and a man who felt so weak that we could not help but be bad. He felt full of remorse for having kept himself from the world of power, I full of guilt for having abandoned the world of love. But the euphoria that we felt at the moment of our separation, of our total personal liberation, dissipated when we both witnessed, impotently, our younger daughter's pain.

Paula sobbed with anguish, inconsolably, during the first days of our migration to Rio de Janeiro. She was flooded by a profound sense of dislocation in this unknown city, which threatened her, as I had chosen it as our place of exile. Omar and I both took responsibility for the cries of this girl who had entered the world as a cry of liberty. She needed a certain sense of security and stability, daily routines that hadn't been present in a house inhabited by two independent people as we had pretended to be. But such routines were essential for her to be able to grow up without fear.

Neither Omar nor I could wholly care for her. Omar could introduce her to the pleasures of Greek mythology and give her affection, but he couldn't ease her external fears: pay for her studies, her health care, or the travels that would let her move eventually to an economically expansive society. I could give her all of that, but I didn't have time to calmly caress away her internal fears. Omar couldn't give me the economic or emotional tranquility I would have needed to embrace Paula peacefully. I didn't give Omar the self-confidence that he needed to work with determination: I didn't make him understand that I would be satisfied with whatever he contributed, or that he could contribute to the standard of living that we both wanted for our daughters. We both felt that we were bad. We felt bad with Paula, bad with each other, bad with ourselves. Our ways of living freely and fully in the world had proven both expensive and uncomfortable; what's more, being free and complete had not brought us the looked-for happiness.

For our daughters' sake, we tried to dance the same choreography of liberal loves but with new steps. We tried to actually live together, rather than simply inhabiting the same house.

Our second act lasted for seven years and, like our first act, it did not have a happy ending. Rancor devoured any possibility of a loving encounter. We discovered that we could neither rely on ourselves nor trust that the other would be there for us. No matter how hard we tried, we could not live in harmony. We stepped on each other's toes all the time.

When I tried to help him by correcting his way of working, he felt that I did not respect him and that I was bad. He reacted, out of his ancestral memory, as a strong man who shouldn't take advice from women. When he tried to recommit himself to his work life, without being distracted by daily domestic issues, I felt abandoned. I reacted like a weak woman, making him feel guilty for his lack of emotional attention.

When I tried to be good, sacrificing my personal progress in order to accommodate his slower pace, he didn't appreciate my efforts, which turned into rage and frustration.

When he tried to be good and to satisfy my desires, I accused him of trying to bribe me with affection in order to hide his inability to compete professionally, to hide the fact that he felt impotent.

We were confused, he and I. We no longer knew when we were bad and when strong; when we were good and when weak; when we should feel guilty and when enraged; when victims and when victors. We didn't know if leaving the other in liberty meant abandoning him, refusing responsibility and commitment, or if the security and care that we wished to give and to receive were invitations to unwanted burials of self or suffocating sacrifices.

Many women like me were proud of our professional identities. But we felt guilty, enraged, ashamed, and poorly defined in our emotional identities. Our multiplicity of feeling confused us and hurt us most in our ways of being mothers.

4

THE IMPRECISE EMBRACE

Paula was four on that autumnal melancholy Saturday morning. Rain fell on the Cristo Redentor, which we could see from the window of our house in Rio de Janeiro, where we lived at the end of the seventies. I did my best in the role of mother-who-plays-with-her-children-in-her-spare-time by watching television with her. An ad showing a tranquil domestic scene appeared on the screen. In this ad, a mother caressed a child who was sitting on her lap. Paula watched this moment more closely than she had watched the cartoons. The next thing I knew, she had scrambled on top of me and was trying to recreate the posture she'd just witnessed. When she managed to do so, she looked at me with something between tenderness and dislocation on her face and said, "I love you very much."

My first reaction was to disqualify the commercial messages that manipulated the emotions using a language of love (as we'd seen in the ad) to gain benefits in the world of power (that of buying and selling, of the media.) I couldn't accept easily that Paula was asking for a simple hug. Wasn't it enough that I waste time watching TV with her? Anyone could do so and, nevertheless, there I was, I who had much more sophisticated and useful ways of showing her love than that provided by a mere caress. I couldn't accept that Paula was asking for a simple hug, but her gesture denounced that my way of embracing her did not provide her with the sense of loving security apparently felt by the kid on TV.

In fact I was barely there with her at all, and Paula could tell that my head was somewhere else. She was used to this. I was off in my busy work life, in my endless problems with Omar, in the demands of others, not with her. My hurried, worried and tense breath did not make likely a trustworthy embrace. But I didn't know that my love would not bring the peace, intimacy or emotional security that Paula asked for.

When my daughters were little, the practice of motherhood was a source of guilt and frustration for me. Do what I might, I felt that I was doing too little, that what I did was not sufficient, that I did it wrong. I ran around like a chicken with my head cut off trying to give them the best of everything. I'd wanted to be a mother but confronted by the demands of these little beings who depended on me—demands I'd not foreseen in my plans of personal progress—I found myself in deep conflict about my new obligations. The consequences of giving life, an act of generous love that had been my free decision as an independent woman, reminded me that I was still enslaved to my family. And this enslavement didn't come from a lack of power but from the requisites of a total love.

On that rainy morning, Paula had caught on to the fact that I loved her while trying not to love her: I hugged her fearing that her hug would asphyxiate me; I looked at her without fixing my gaze on her for fear that I would then stop regarding the rest of the world. This contradictory kind of love left unforeseen and unwanted droughts in my daughters. Like other women of their generation, they suffer from emotional lacks even greater and more difficult to resolve than the romantic miss-encounters of their grandmothers and mothers. Some of the daughters of we women who knew how to conquer the world of power feel that they are utterly hopeless in the world of love.

This affirmation is not a *mea culpa*. Neither is it a confession, a sign of repentance, nor a request for pardon. I loved my daughters, but I lost myself going back and forth between my emotional incoherences inherited from my parents. Those peregrinations confused my daughters.

Recognizing that my incoherent way of embracing my daughters caused them great confusion in the realm of intimate emotions, I repeat the gesture my mother made when she shared with me her certainty that her insufficient embrace didn't make me feel sure of myself in the public sphere.

My mother, seeing me at twelve provoking the school authorities or become too defiant for my current resources, said to me: "I can't take care of you. I feel like a mother hen who has hatched an eagle egg. My wings don't let me go so high, I can't protect you. I don't know how to teach you to avoid the dangers of skies I don't recognize nor can I accompany you." Her voice didn't sound angry. I didn't realize that she was sad not to know how to keep me from harming myself. I listened to her words as if they were a sentence condemning me to be alone in the world. To feel *untouchable* hurt but, more than anything, this idea disconcerted me. How was it possible that she, who gave me life, could not teach me how to live? I blamed myself: surely the problem was that I was too strange, too crazy, too sour for my mother's world. Feeling that she rejected me, I scorned her help and for a long time I rejected her insufficient embrace entirely.

For years I believed that these misunderstandings and faulty encounters came from a lack of love. I thought that my mother didn't understand me because she didn't love me enough. I was angry at her because her embrace could not contain me properly, but I also felt guilty because I refused every single one of her attempts to draw close to me again: I did not love her enough either. Her advice struck me as trivial, ridiculous, naive; inadequate. My mother embarrassed me. How could I be held by an embrace that I myself discounted?

I was fifteen the time they called her into school with me. I had disobeyed some rule and, once more, found myself in a complicated situation. I was scared and I felt under-protected by her; I thought that she would not know how to defend me from unjust accusations as well as would—or so I thought then—my father. While we mounted the stairs to the school entrance, I asked her not to talk: I was scared that she would say something stupid. For the first time in my life she hit me.

My mother slapped my face and with her words taught me permanently the meaning of dignity: "I will not allow you to disown me. I will not allow you to treat me like a babysitter paid by your father. I'm your mother and here I am, at your side. I always gave you the best of myself. And if you don't like what I give you, that doesn't mean that I'm not good enough."

My surprise, happiness, and pride in feeling that in her way she did embrace me erased the pain of the slap. My mother had recognized that it was hard for her to understand me, but she wouldn't let me accuse her of abandonment. She had shown me that it was I who rejected her: if I chose not to confide in her, I could not blame her for my feeling of loneliness. Her gesture made me understand, many years later and with the help of my own daughters, that my mother was good, not stupid.

My mother devalued herself socially but she knew that she loved me. Her embrace had been insufficient, true, but not weak: the slap showed me the force of her love. Without that, I would only have seen what both of us considered her intellectual weakness.

My mother pushed me into skies higher than her own. It was inevitable that she be unable to contain me properly if I managed to reach such heights. Making clear to me that she could not cover for me made clear as well that I'd separated myself from her, that I lived in other worlds, other vital spaces, other emotional horizons. She also in this way gave me permission to live my life at a higher speed and stronger power than she had, that I invent my own way of being in this world where my father lived but that my mother only glimpsed now and then curiously. But her invitation made me feel abandoned, that she gave up her maternal responsibility, that she left me alone.

The feeling of not fitting into one's mother's arms, of not being contained by her womb, is a terrifying one. It's hard to imagine that the woman who gave us life cannot sustain us in our identity by embracing us as we wish to be embraced. The immediate and logical response is to become infuriated: we learn early how to fight against the pain of these lacks of embrace. But the fighting only produces an ephemeral and fleeting sigh of relief; the anger increases the sense of emptiness and solitude.

I'd pulled away from my mother, and that day, ascending the staircase at school, my mother did something that made me able to realize, years later, that I was not asking for too much, just as she was not offering too little. We were different, we didn't live in the same world, we each had our own language. Increasing my demands or exaggerating her response couldn't correct our feeling that we did not fit one another properly.

Later my daughters got angry with me and for a long time rejected me. Not because they found my embrace insufficient, but because they found it contradictory, ambiguous, conflicted, unpredictable. Sometimes they were embarrassed by me, sometimes afraid of me. They didn't see me as weak and stupid but rather as bad and authoritarian.

I didn't caress them as the woman on TV caressed her child. I didn't want to be dishonest, and I knew that intimacy wasn't easy for me. They accused me of being too hard, not affectionate enough. My honesty was cruelty when it showed them that they weren't the be-all and end-all of my life; my honesty provoked guilt in them when I showed the pain I felt at their aggression. In public, I countered their accusations; in private I cried from shame at not knowing how to be a mother.

My maternal embrace, like that of others of my generation, was intermittent, spasmodic, ambiguous, but not purposefully bad. I wanted my daughters to inhabit the best of all possible worlds: I thought myself to be complete and as such I thought I could give my daughters a complete embrace. At the time I felt bad but I thought it was due to the small amount of time I spent with them. I didn't know that my way of being a mother had been established by my emotional contradictions, nor that my daughters would inherit the conflict—as well as a sense of powerlessness over it—between desires to see me as good and as strong at once.

This is not a confession of guilt. But it is an acceptance of responsibility: in trying to show my daughters how to be both women and people, I've transmitted my own conflicts to them. I wanted to teach them how to be complete women but I contributed to their growing up as contradictory women. My way of loving them exposed them to the risk of being cast off from themselves as they searched, without knowing how or where, for the most complete, best, fullest embrace.

When my mother urged me to liberate myself from masculine domination and to transform myself into a strong person in the public sphere, she didn't imagine that, by appropriating the arms of power I would inevitably change my ideas about feminine goodness, my ways of loving, and my emotional necessities. When I urged my daughters to seek the best in the worlds of power and love at the same time, I didn't imagine that they would inevitably change their ways of loving and their emotional necessities. I didn't foresee that my contradictory messages would leave them without clear signposts, navigating in waters strange to all of us, headed towards emotional horizons that became less intelligible with each passing day. I didn't imagine that, in my urging them to seek the best of everything, I would condemn them to wander like emotional nomads, pilgrims eternally searching for the perfect love, driven by the utopian idea of a state of complete emotional satiety. I didn't know how to teach them the difference between appetite and voracity, between wanting to win and wanting to triumph, between enthusiasm for life's adventures and excitement about the dangers of death.

By devaluing their professional and intellectual capacities, my mother and other women of her generation ended up devaluing themselves in general, denying the value of their way of loving us. Thus they contaminated their feminine legacy; they gave us the idea that their love was weak. Without meaning to, they also ensured that this model, in which loyalty and weakness were joined, left as an alternative for some of us a model in which was joined strength and badness.

In my generation, we contaminated our legacies by devaluing our ways of caring for our children. Feeling that we embraced them more with guilt than with pleasure, more with obligation than with happiness, as if completing a task rather than because we had the right to embrace them, we contaminated our legacy: we transmitted to them the idea of our love as bad and weak. Our way of valuing ourselves in the professional world while devaluing ourselves in the emotional world gave them the idea that, for strong women such as them and us, the former was valuable and the latter, dangerous.

My mother and I were different from each other; my daughters and I are different too. Natasha and Paula's world isn't the world I lived in at their age: the men who might be their partners aren't the same as those we looked for; my daughters' vital needs are different from my own. The verb *to love* as much as the verb *to be able to*, the concepts of family and partnership as much as the concepts of power and ambition, acquire different meanings in different historical and cultural moments, in different ethnic groups and social groupings. My mother and I, my daughters and I, are different from one another.

So far, we are all born from wombs. But the work of differentiating ourselves and of knowing ourselves to be different from those who gave birth to us is more complicated for daughters than for sons. We come from the same and we seem the same; as such, we think that we are the same as and must feel the same as our mothers. By contrast, the first glance at sons puts them in the place of someone other, different. Sons have not only the permission but the familiar mandate to think, to feel, and to act distinctly from their mothers.

Daughters seem to offer their mothers an infallible antidote to the feeling of solitude. Being the same, we foment mutually the fantasy of an embrace that would promise unconditional and total fusion. When this illusion turns out to be just that, illusory, we confront the knowledge of limits that includes the understanding of death. No one—not our daughters, not our mothers, can restore to us the edenic embrace that both enjoyed before our births. For love of life, for a mother's love of her daughter, birth is produced. The new being comes into light and the happiness of growth but also into solitude and confrontation, to the pain of decisions and mistakes. For love of the mother and of the daughter, the womb, unique universe, must expulse and its guest must leave. For love of our daughters, we mothers push them away from ourselves. For love of us, some daughters obey and leave us. Strange love that demands solitude. Severe love that requires the renunciation of intimacy between two people who love each other. Painful love that condemns to nostalgia the embrace that pushed us from the nest.

My mother gave me permission to abandon her and to betray her ways of being a woman. Her loving way of telling me that her love was insufficient let me obey her mandate of progressing in the world, differentiating myself from her and creating for myself a new identity as a professional woman, but I didn't, despite her urgings, create a new way of loving.

When my daughters were born, Natasha in 1970 and Paula in 1974, I'd completed my path into the professional world. I didn't work as the weak one in the home of my strong husband, as I thought my mother had done. Neither did I occupy myself as a well-educated governess for the children of the patriarchy, as I thought Mario had proposed that I do. I had transformed myself into a professional, with liberty, independence, and power. I was myself when I worked, when I occupied social spaces, when I progressed in the world of work. But I didn't know how to be myself in the world of family affection, and, especially, in the world of motherhood.

My mother had lived at home with little autonomy and scant personal liberty. I remember her, silent and solitary, cooking for when my father would come home from work and my older brothers from school, cooking so that everything would be impeccably prepared. I also remember the meals, the comforting steam of them, the house as a haven, shelter from the torments and fears that threatened from outside. The house protected. Still, *inside* remains contaminated, in my memory, with a negative idea of quiescence. The house suffocated us. Like many women of my generation, I associated *domestic* with *domesticated*, with feelings of emptiness, passive depression, apathy and lack of interest.

When we were mothers, some women of my generation neither inhabited ourselves nor wished our daughters to inhabit the sad *inside* world in which, we thought, our mothers had lived. We'd learned that, according to the terms of traditional emotional codes, the house filled with sound, motion and life only when the man came home. He brought news of the powerful outside world of which the woman was ignorant and which she couldn't see from the kitchen. Public space and social situations evoked images of vitality, of important activities, of transcendent exchanges, that attracted me as much as Paula was attracted by the domestic scene on TV.

I lived in this *outside* world and I wanted my daughters to live in it too. I brought them with me everywhere from the time they were born so that they would learn how to be independent, so that they would neither suffer as my mother had not done nor waste time as I had. I wanted them to know how to think as adults even when they were little girls. I imitated my mother, transmitting to them a greater valuation of the world of power. I surpassed my mother when I taught them to scorn and to fear intimacy, when I gave them a monotonous and scornful image of the world of love.

Like many of my contemporaries, I thought that I was teaching my daughters how to embrace life: how to move towards the future. I didn't know, and neither did many of my contemporaries, that the motor of this motion was located in the past: in the fear of inertia, the fear of feeling oneself to be a passive and dependent woman, of being trapped in the traditional morals of emotional security. Thinking that I was giving them a passion for living transcendently, existing for something or for someone, always in motion, always moving forward, in fact I taught them that immanence, existing in oneself and for oneself, in contemplation, is dangerous.

Our way of trying to be Superwoman, capable of having everything, taught our daughters to flee from death, to flee constantly from the idea of depression tied to the image of the woman-who-waits-for-her-husband-to-get-home. Watching us live, our daughters could not but gain the impression that doing is more important than being. One of the unlooked for consequences of our form of progressive parenting was that the struggle against feminine passivity took the form of frenetic activities in our daughters' generation; our rage at not being listened to took the form of their never hearing anything; our will to make our voices heard took the form of their refusal of silence, itself a necessary condition for dialogue.

Many of us had as partners men who, like my brother, had learned the language of the world of love from their mothers. With time, their embraces gave our daughters the tenderness that our embraces lacked. Our daughters and sons thus learned the language of power from their mothers and that of love from their fathers. An unforeseen result has been that many of our children see women as the stronger sex and men as the kinder.

I didn't make my daughters into the be-all and end-all of my life, as my mother had done with me; and, in not giving up my life for them, I gave them their own lives; I believed that children shouldn't be their parents' property. In time this idea turned into another idea, another unwanted consequence of our good intentions: children were no longer their parents' responsibility.

We tried to liberate ourselves from our mothers' idea of love as possessive. We liberated ourselves from all forms of commitment whatsoever. We believed in free love, without realizing that this mandate could turn out to mean that to be free one could not love: love binds, creates dependence and kills liberty. Love works as ballast.

The dictionary defines ballast thus: "stones, sand or other weighty material used to submerge a ship to the proper point and to guarantee successful navigation." For us, ballast became synonymous with obstacle, blockade, and the word is still used to refer to anything that impedes the pleasure of a vertiginous and limitless motion.

A close relationship with one's parents could work as ballast if it truncated the total liberty that the young people of my time wanted. The family had revealed itself as a patriarchal structure that limited women's options and so we women feared that children would rob of us of the time needed for the personal realization that, in the sixties, we equated with professional realization.

Some of us wanted to distinguish ourselves for our intellectual capacity rather than for our beauty or our domestic skills. We thought that looking for the meaning of life in our relationships with our husbands or children was opting for a minor and secondary life project.

We tried to harmonize our decisions to develop ourselves professionally with our obligations to marry and have children—mandate we had received from our mothers and obeyed without question, in order to be normal women, socially integrated, without the instability of an empty or flexible emotional life. And so when I embraced my children I thought more of my needs than of their own.

To give my daughters a better feminine model than the one with which I had grown up, I didn't dedicate myself only to them; I wanted them to grow up with the understanding that "woman" was not synonymous with "mother" or "wife." I wanted them, when they were grown, to define themselves from within, rather than in relation to others, even when these others were their own husbands or children. I wanted them to be owners of themselves, independent as I had been, but even freer. But, although such was not my intention, my daughters' obedience to these mandates has left them at risk of floundering in a sea of confused feelings, free but alone, owners of themselves exhausted from bearing all the weight of their own lives.

My mother shortened the emotional distances between herself and others so much that she fused with them, confused herself with them: her legacy taught me to look closely, to discover and to value the details that, like keys, open onto people's inner lives. My father spoke of the human history writ large and of the need to understand the world and its inhabitants from an impersonal perspective: from him I learned to consider from a distance, to observe the large organizational schemes in which individual feelings almost disappeared. I lived shortening and lengthening emotional distances at the same time.

Two equally absurd scenes illustrate my difficulty finding and maintaining the proper distance between my daughters and myself, a distance both short, so that they felt understood and accompanied, and long, so that they didn't feel smothered or invaded.

I carried Paula at my hip until she was two. And I was so used to her weight at my hip that one day, leaving a taxi, I had a moment of desperation thinking that I had lost her, until I realized that I was still carrying her, there where she always was. Paula was an extension of my body, part of me. We were fused, welded: the too-short emotional distance I had learned from my mother was repeating itself in my link to my daughters. They and I lived in one time and space, we were one. I had tried to avoid exactly this way of relating to them.

Another time, arriving a half-hour late to pick up the girls from their English classes, I ran while fixated on my reflections about maternal responsibilities. I was so absorbed in my guilt that I ran past my daughters three times without seeing them. The too-great emotional distance I had learned from my father made me think of my daughters as abstract tasks to be accomplished, rather than as human beings.

If I got too close, if I began to see the little signals they gave off that showed me how much and in what ways they needed me, I felt suffocated, a prisoner of the need to take care of them. The fear of sacrificing personal liberty by assuming maternal responsibility made me flee from my own children. I tried to make my flight ever easier by assuming more and more professional responsibilities.

When I lived in the world of power, I felt strong and I forgot the rest of my life. Until I left some professional scene or argument frazzled or worn out or badly hurt and found myself very far from home. Then, feeling the lack of that unconditional embrace one expects from the family, I ran home as if to a refuge, seeking comfort from my daughters' hugs while thinking that *I* was comforting *them*. That they were not complicit in my self-delusion and did not receive my affectionate gestures whenever and however I wanted hurt me: they were bad and ungrateful because that did not let me feel *good* as I needed to. Paula showed me this incongruence when, on one of these difficult days, after receiving many hours of her attention, I returned to my own preoccupations. She said: "I kept you company because I knew you were sad. And now that you've gotten a phone call you leave me alone, without asking me if I need you? I stopped playing with my friends to be with you, but you don't stop working to be with me."

It hurts me to confess that I had to hide my fear of being alone with my children during the nanny's day off. I was so scared of not knowing how to entertain them and of boring them that I filled out time together with constant activity. I guarded myself so much from their pleading little faces, for fear of not knowing how to decipher them that I never even understood what they asked of me.

In the Buenos Aires of that time, some professional women stayed home with their children in the mornings and took them to the neighborhood playground. I avoided this ritual as if I feared being poisoned by it. I felt bad if I met colleagues there: I didn't like my daughters to see my professional competencies and insecurities. I felt bad if I met housewives there: I didn't like my daughters to see my maternal insecurities and incompetence. In any one of these scenes, I felt out of place, as if I did not fit in. I didn't know how to be a mother from within my professional identity; I didn't know how to act. Many daughters of women of my age complain that we acted falsely with them: one way when we were alone with them and another utterly different way when we were in the presence of others. But we were not false: simply, we didn't know how to behave—we lacked useful models of motherhood. As we didn't know how to take on the role of mothers, because we defined ourselves as professionals, we tried out various attitudes and postures, looking for the one that would best serve in the maternal scene.

I did this trying out, this rehearsal, by offering my daughters a preposterous number of activities. My mother once scolded me because, recently returned from a business trip that had kept me away from home for over a week, I wanted to take my girls to an amusement park. I ignored my own tiredness but, more importantly, I closed my eyes to their interest in becoming re-acquainted with me after this separation. I wanted distraction, not them; I wanted to distract myself from them, from the tension that caring for them caused me.

I also tried to be a mother by pushing them into other peoples' embraces: their grandmother's, their nanny's, their father's, in that order. I feared that they would not like the embrace I offered them. My body was not like that of the woman in the TV ad that Paula wished for us to imitate; neither was it soft and curvy like that of the grandmother who knew how to caress them and how to take away their night terrors. I educated my girls, but their babysitter and their father played with them and entertained them. I could offer them the festive exciting world that teaches how to do, but not the peaceful slow world that teaches how to be. I did not know how to create a space for us, one in which to listen to the intimate murmurs that unfurl themselves over time. So little did I trust my own way of living in the world of the emotions that I taught my daughters not to confide in me and not to expect my embrace.

For fear of feeling that I was only a hole—a shadowy dark nook, full of sadness and frustrations, as I imagined my mother had been—I tried to be a shining sword, resplendent with successes and ambition. I felt that I was a woman of both forms. I went from feeling like a powerful person, one who knew the best way to educate my daughters so that they esteemed their own values, to feeling absolutely incapable of calming my daughters' anguishes, as I succumbed all the time to my own. From these two modalities of being, I embraced my daughters. They learned and feared both feelings.

My mother preferred being the one who loved, cared for and worried about others. Needing a man's love would have been her Achilles' heel, the vulnerable spot where my father could harm her. She knew how to erect barriers that kept her emotionally invulnerable. She got used to thinking that receiving love wasn't important. Without realizing it, I learned from her this form of invulnerability: to not need love seemed a good survival strategy for some women of my generation.

I tried to make my daughters into women who were strong not only in the world of power, as my mother had wanted me to be, but also in the world of love. I wanted their emotional lives to be entirely unrestricted. But, in my rush to give my daughters total embraces, I gave them intermittent and contradictory embraces. My way of living in two worlds—that of power and that of love—had as consequence my daughters' possible inheritance of such contradiction. Sometimes they act as if they think that only if they are bad can they freely enjoy their personal time and their own space, and that if they are weak can they confess their needs for dependence on an adequate embrace.

Absolute self-sufficiency and independence is a heavy weapon to carry. Some women of my daughters' generation don't know how to need someone else without feeling contemptuous of themselves. When they run out of the necessary strength to keep maintaining their armor of independence—either against their fear of not being loved or against their guilt at not knowing how to love—some of them draw a connection with their emotional needs and see themselves as powerless sieves, contemptibly dependent, contemptibly "feminine." They idealize a love that requires them to find men who will make them feel loved and lovable, and then protest indignantly when they feel vulnerable because they love.

Some women of my mother's generation gave their daughters a mandate to be loyal to the truth, but this loyalty turned out to be more bearable for them than for us, because they responded to a sole truth. Their existences were defined by and for their families, by and for their children; all they thought, did or felt had to cohere with such existence. Their ambition was to be the best within the world of love.

Some women of my generation maintained a double system of coherencies, under the terms of which we had to be loyal to two truths: we wanted to have a family which loved us and which we loved, and to define ourselves as lovable women; at the same time, we wanted to have a respected profession and to define ourselves as respectable professionals. We sought liberty and independence along with familiar security and protection: we urged ourselves to be both strong and good in the worlds of both power and love.

Strong women married to weak men dreamed of husbands or lovers whose strength would match their own; weak women married to bad men dreamed of husbands and lovers whose goodness would match their own. In the topsy-turvy, crisscrossed world of our emotions, in the sixties and seventies, we were never completely happy in our relationships. In compensation, we alternated over time or juxtaposed in space between these two ways of loving. But divorcing one man and marrying another, like maintaining relationships with two different men at once, did not bring us happiness. We remained, no matter what changes we tried to make, trapped in our own contradictory emotions: we neither loved nor felt ourselves loved wholly and coherently.

Those of us who managed to define ourselves happily as professionals mandated that our daughters mimic our model of professional success while surpassing our emotional failures. Progress, for this generation, means not only being a professional woman but also at the same time being successful in love. There is no longer one truth, as there was for their grandmothers; nor are there two truths, as there were for their mothers. Young women today are faced with demand to be loyal to multiple truths, those derived from crossing the rules of the professional world with the rules of the emotional world. The task submerges them in a confusion in which they argue, uselessly, over which is the truest truth. How can they find true love if they want various loves? How can they know which is the best relationship, if they don't even know the criteria by which they might choose it or the means by which they might recognize it?

Perhaps the contradictory embraces they received from us, explain, in part, why young women jump from one extreme to the other, motivated by the constant doubt that accompanies their search for perfection. Perhaps our contradictory embraces explain why sometimes young women seem not to need anything from anyone and sometimes seem to need far too much from everyone; why sometimes they humiliate others and sometimes feel humiliated; why sometimes they abandon others and sometimes are abandoned; why sometimes they mistreat their partners and sometimes are themselves mistreated. Perhaps our embraces explain why sometimes they embrace others as if they themselves were violent men and sometimes ask to be embraced as if they were scared little girls; why sometimes they demand an embrace as if it were owed them and sometimes beg for affection as if they only deserved crumbs.

Perhaps our contradictory embraces explain why our daughters never know when they are good or bad, when they are strong or weak, in their relationships. Perhaps our contradictions explain why, already in their third decade of life, our daughters fear that they were born condemned to drag their confused emotions along with them forever, on an undecipherable path of partial and divided loves.

5

Split Loves

Lena, the Mexican journalist who blamed the women of our generation for not having taught those of her generation to love, asked herself:

"How come no one ever told me that you need a graduate degree to understand men? I can't talk to a man, tell him what's happening to me and sense that he understands me. I don't have this problem in other parts of my life: I never feel as inept as I do in relationships. I don't know what I'm doing wrong. I feel full of love. Why don't I meet someone who wants to accept what I can offer?"

Alessandra, the as intelligent as beautiful Italian lawyer, complains:

"At work I get what I want, but I can't find a man who gives me what I need. The ones who understand me don't want to marry a woman like me; they prefer girls who don't think so much. The ones who want to marry me don't understand me and think I'm too complicated. I'm not a typical housewife but I'm not a typical executive either. Do I have to lop off parts of myself to fit into some mold? When I don't define myself according to the existing patterns I feel that for men I don't exist: I am not, no one sees me."

In my mother's time, daughters surpassed their mothers by becoming stronger and more successful in the world of love, by being better than their mothers were. In my time, daughters surpassed their mothers by strengthening themselves in the world of power, by being stronger than their mothers. Those of us who wanted to progress professionally navigated between two well-defined and delimited continents: we left our mothers' domestic territories and set out for our fathers' professional territories. To reach our destination meant to travel from one port to another.

Women of my generation wanted our daughters to surpass us in romantic and domestic happiness. We wanted them to find men both strong and good with whom they might have the love that eluded their mothers. Convinced that they are the best, our daughters believe that they should be the best lovers; women who best know how to love. But instead they feel more than incompetent, more than emotionally stunted: they are anguished when they don't understand what has happened to them, when they find themselves lost among the splintered fragments of the split loves they learned from their mothers, when they don't know how to love as they believe they ought to do. Our daughters feel strongly contradictory and strongly dispersed: they cannot prioritize their desires nor needs, they swim in a rough sea of option and indecision, possibility and error.

Lena and Alessandra's voices and other women like them express the same sensation of abysm and of stultifying uncertainty. They don't know what they urgently need and want to know: what path they must take to be more successful—here, happier—than their mothers, in their intimate relationships.

How do women of my daughters' generation surpass their mothers? The options open to them are much more confused than for previous generations. If they choose one way of loving, they renounce the others; if they choose certain emotional advantages, they lose others; if they avoid certain emotional disadvantages, they suffer from others. The crossing is harder: there isn't a line that leads directly from their emotional chaos to a complex emotional order. They navigate most often in circles or in crazy zigzags, floundering between the ways of loving taught by the professional sphere and those taught by the personal. But no port of entry delivers them to all of their wishes, no definition represents them entirely. Drowning in their own contradictions, they become emotional shipwrecks or nomads.

The same does not happen in the workplace. There, they know themselves to be dignified heiresses of the tradition begun by their mothers. They are as strong and as good as we are, if not more so. At work, they use their intelligence as much as their sensibility; they use strong thoughts as much as good feelings; they use practical reasoning as much as intangible intuiting; they use the rapidity of expert hunters as much as the caution of dedicated reapers. And in this they are not alone. Stronger men, those who have at their disposal all necessary resources and who do not need anyone's help in order to do as they like, know that they should care about and concern themselves with others' needs and desires. Everyone, men and women alike, who wants to advance in the professional sphere, knows that one must be good as well as strong. The ideology of the power of love has gained so many skilled adherents that stronger people must also be better people: those who better serve their consultants are better able to serve themselves and to expand their businesses.

But our daughters have inherited more than the advantages of being good in the public sphere. They have inherited as well the disadvantages of being strong in the private sphere: they act as if being friendly is the opposite of being authentic, being attentive the opposite of being attended to, caring for another the opposite of being cared for; as if, emotionally, doing what one wants is the opposite of doing what the other wants. Our daughters act as if they believed that loving is the opposite of being loved. Their relationships with men can illuminate with a ferocious virulence the conflict between the designated winners in the world of power and those in the world of love.

Some women of my daughters' generation learned the vocabularies and practices of divided and oppositional loves from watching their mothers live. Others learned by observing the advantages and disadvantages of split loves in their parents' contradictory attitudes. (The parent who taught them nurture could not exercise force; the parent who taught them how to fight did not know how to nurture.) These attitudes became irreconcilable oppositions within the daughters. They believe, for example, that someone who knows how to defend himself does not know how to love and that someone who knows how to love does not know how to defend himself. Other women of my daughters' generation speak of an unbridgeable chasm between their parents' emotional ideology, which valued nurture and loyalty, and that of their friends and peers, which values force. Those women who learned to believe in both ways of loving think that if they do what they want they are betraying those who love them, while if they do what others want, they are betraying themselves.

These women learned split loves in various schools, but all split loves—and the students of such loves—share the same contradictions, the same confusions, the same sufferings. They aspire to win and to progress emotionally, and they want to enjoy the advantages offered by all kinds of love, at the same time and with the same intensity. They are not content with enjoying successively or in juxtaposition all of their various options. Neither divorce nor adultery strikes them as a desirable option. But in their relationships, when they are strong they feel that they are bad, and when they are good, they feel that they are weak.

They navigate always and in anguish between one way and another of experiencing love, between two contradictory and divergent emotional modalities.

1. Between dependence and independence

Natasha and I didn't manage to regulate the emotional distances between us. She wanted the freedom to sleep away from home whenever she wanted but I didn't have the same freedom to dispose of her room—in my house—as I wanted. She wanted me to listen attentively to her tales of romantic foibles but when I asked how she was she accused me of invading her privacy. The most contradictory situation happened when she moved in with a university friend. Thinking that she wanted this situation very much, I helped her move and hid my anguish: I felt rejected by her because she chose not to live with me. In the Buenos Aires of the late eighties liberations and repressions went hand in hand: women didn't leave their parents' home only to get married. They did so also to study or to work outside the country, but not to live on their own. To my enormous surprise, Natasha became depressed—her sister told me later—because I hadn't cried or tried to make her stay: she thought it didn't matter to me that she was living away from her family, on her own. She thought this was a sign of my lack of love for her, as she had learned that in our circle of strong and liberated women, family was still taken as a primary priority, even though we would not confess as much publicly. I did not understand her, she did not understand me. I never knew when I was holding her too closely or not closely enough. I didn't know how to put my arms around her; she, how to put her arms around me.

Psychoanalysis was very in vogue in my country when my daughters were born. And as a profession it criticized births that were too easy or quick as demonstrating that the mother wanted to get rid of the child. But difficult or long labors were also bad, as they demonstrated the mother's desire to retain the child.

With this inheritance of split loves, women like my daughters feel that in every relationship they gain something they want and lose something they need. "If he doesn't want me in his life, I don't want myself; my life is in his hands." Thus they suffer when they opt for the advantages of emotional dependence. "Because I don't need anyone, people think I don't need love; my life is in my hands alone." Thus they suffer when they opt for the advantages of emotional independence. They always fear that they have opted for the wrong choice. They are terrorized by the fear of disappearing in a protective embrace if they give in to their own need for love and security; at the same time, they are terrorized that all affection and connection will vanish if they give in to their need to remain without affective ballast or bonds.

Andrea, an Argentinean economist born in the 70's who completed her post-graduate studies in one of the best American universities and later decided to live in Manhattan because of the attractive professional opportunities that this place offers, describes her current situation: "My mother struggles against men's power. I have power in the world; professionally, my life is much better than that of many of peers, but I feel that my public success works against success in my love life. If a man wants me, I see myself as an object and that makes me angry. If he doesn't consult with me, even if it's because he wants to surprise me with something nice, I get angry because I think he's invasive and doesn't respect my needs. But when a man responds to my wishes I think he's too submissive and has no personality."

Some women of my daughters' generation flee from relationships that encourage emotional dependence and therefore threaten them with suffocation while also fearing relationships that encourage emotional independence and therefore threaten them with abandonment. They want to nourish themselves with the protective security promoted by the traditional way of understanding gender roles, while at the same time and with the same intensity they want to benefit from the enriching liberty offered by the new ways of understanding.

They have learned from an early age how to dance choreographies of split loves: they want an embrace that offers the safety of unconditional security while also wanting an embrace that offers the exhilaration of unconditional liberty. They long for an embrace that would guarantee them complete and eternal care and at the same time for one that would ask nothing of them.

They want a relationship that would provide for them and satisfy all their desires but they are bothered when they feel that they need someone. They fear that dependence will make them feel obligated to do what the other wants: to obey, even to obey the loving suggestions posed by care, security, and protection, strikes them as humiliating. To let themselves be told what to do strikes them as too high a price to pay for the security they desire.

They want to be free and to be able to satisfy their desires on their own but they also worry that independence condemns them to being alone: doing what they want requires liberating themselves from every tie that might oppose or obstruct their decisions. Not to count on anyone, not to trust anyone but themselves, strikes them as too painful a price for the liberty for which they long.

Lovingly dependent or powerfully independent? Cared for and submissive or abandoned and free? How could we teach our daughters which embrace was the better one if we ourselves did not know?

Women who don't escape the vicious circle of emotional contradiction don't know how, where, or in what way to search for a relationship that would allow them to be both dependent and independent at once.

2. Between fusion and individuation

Some women of my daughters' generation want to fuse themselves with the other at the same time and with the same intensity as they want to differentiate themselves from him. For these women, to individuate—to be oneself—is an urgent necessity, one that cannot be negotiated.

And so the longed-for fusions threaten them; they fear that they will stop being themselves. But so do the longed-for individuations threaten them; they fear that they will be trapped in an isolated island of selfhood.

"Who am *I*, how do I know when I am *myself*, when there are so many ways of being *I* in which I feel that I am *myself*?" Ask women like my daughters.

They have learned from a very young age to dream of unconditional absolute love, of the blissful peace of those who live in a fused fissureless way. Simultaneously, they have learned to dream of another idealized love, another illusion: that in which people live in individuated happiness and strength, without compromises. These women long for the absence of conflict and believe that emotional peace only comes from one half of the couple disappearing. Either, for love of the other, they disappear, or else, for love of self, they make the other disappear.

I am not the only mother, nor my daughters the only women who believe that the best way of avoiding conflict is when there is only one voice emitted at a time. We didn't know how to talk: neither them nor us heard what we didn't want to hear. Our daughters learned from their mothers that, when two persons talk at the same time, there is no dialogue. They believed that a good dialogue consisted in the simultaneous emission of two efficient monologues: the monologue of fusion and that of individuation. We taught them that there exist two homogenous monolithic coherent discourses, opposed to one another but each cogent in itself.

The monologue of loving fusion affirms: we are, we feel, we think, and we want the same. It promotes the absence of conflict by making mute the *I*, by renouncing any vestige of individual desire and personal existence.

The monologue of powerful individuation affirms: I know what I feel; want, think, and desire and I also know what the other feels, wants, thinks, and desires. It promotes the absence of conflict by making mute the *we*, by allowing one and only one *I* to make all the decisions, assuming all responsibility in this same action.

Not to speak or not to listen, to accept or to impose with shouts the desire and the voice of one half of a couple, promotes the solid hegemony of an infallible truth while also guaranteeing an utter lack of communication. Like the monologue of fusion, the monologue of individuation offers peace, but also a solitary silence.

Women of my daughters' generation learned that one had to know how to listen and how to obey in order to win in the world of love, but also that one had to know how to shout and to give orders in order to win in the world of power. In this emotional confusion, they wanted the peace that silence brings but they feared the attendant solitude; they wanted the triumph of the soliloquy but they feared the attendant emotional poverty. They believe that they know how to speak and that the other does not want to hear them. They believe that by shouting they can make themselves heard. Until they discover that their shouts only receive silence as an answer. They don't know when to hold their tongue or when to shout; they don't know how to engage in dialogue.

Some women of my daughters' generation suffer because they still don't know how, where, or in what way to look for the grammar of the *I/you/we*; they don't know how to speak of the self and the other at the same time and with the same intensity.

3.   Between the expected and the unexpected

Some women of my daughters' generation want the stable emotional links promised by the power of love as well as the constant innovation of new brief relationships as promised by the love of power. So they reject the suffocating sameness of stable relationships as the same time as they fear the fragility of newly formed unions.

They have learned since they were little to value relationships that offer guarantees of belonging and mutual commitment. The rites and traditions of permanent love function for them as an extraordinary antidote to the insecurities caused by a world in which events happen, a world always in flux. They know that wealth—not only economic but also that of social recognition, familiar networks and friendship—require a life situation that is stable, trustworthy and predictable. At the same time, they have learned to value emotional relationships that let them forge a new kind of link in each encounter and that surprise them with novelty. They have learned to desire unknown, exotic, exciting encounters. They know that wealth requires a life situation that is flexible, open to change, and able to accept the risk of not controlling everything.

To stay or to leave, to keep or to change, to put down roots or to disperse oneself; earth or air; the old known or the new unknown; a bird in the hand or two in the bush—thus the women of my daughters' generation question themselves over and over.

Natasha complained that I wasn't a mother like those of her friends: I didn't pick her up after school; I didn't dress or speak like those other mothers. But she was also proud that I was different, that I organized things and said things that those other mothers would not say. When I confessed to her my guilt at not having given her a stable routine life, she consoled me by saying that she would never have wanted such a boring life. But when I spoke to her of the advantages of the diverse life experiences to which I'd exposed her, she chastised me for not attending to the anxiety that these experiences caused her. Neither she nor I knew which of my contradictory ways of being was "the best," with which *I* she should identify herself, which *myself* she should imitate.

Some women like her learned to want the happiness promised by a lifelong love as well as the happiness promised by a love that changes every day. They learned to want the powerful happiness of someone who conquers newly each day and the loving happiness of someone who keeps, conquered for all time, a single partner.

In the fragmentation of their feelings, they become bored when they find themselves trapped in a love relationship that is stable but also unchanging. They become angry with themselves when, for fear of being alone, they content themselves with the repetitive predictable anodynically inoffensive embrace offered by bureaucratic loves. But they become scared if they find themselves trapped in loves that are exciting and volatile. They become angry with themselves when, for fear of being alone, they pursue the unpredictable changeful seductively dangerous embrace offered by unstable loves. As they eroticize danger, so they banalize tenderness, and do not know with what to content themselves.

Andrea has been in a stable relationship for several months.

She says: "I want Bill to leave me alone for awhile. I need time for myself. It's suffocating to have to see him or talk to him every day, to have to repeat the same questions and answers. The more he looks at me and the more he tells me he loves me, the less I like it. But when he gets angry because I treat him poorly and it seems that he will leave me, I become desperate. I ask him for forgiveness. He forgives me. And everything goes back to the same boring routine. Bill is a delightful person but I don't love him as a man, as I do Peter, the man who mistreated me for three years—I'm still in love with him. Am I a masochist? Do I not tolerate happiness and wellness? Is my mother right when she says that no man can give me what I want because I'm too complicated and demanding?"

Some women of my daughters' generation don't know how, where, or in what way to look for a relationship that would offer them both permanent emotional security and innovative emotional liberty. They fear that such a relationship is impossible. They begin to believe that they will therefore never find it.

4. Between politeness and frankness

Some women of my daughters' generation want both courtesy and frankness in their relationships. So they reject courtesies and friendliness that strike them as obsequious as much as they fear cruelties embedded in honest and bravely truthful phrases.

As much as they want a cordial daily life, one full of little attentions and mutual gratitude, they also fear that too much care is a manifestation of the typical servile personality of a hypocritical or submissive person. But they don't know how to distinguish between friendliness and courtesy on the one hand and the simple fear of defending their own truths on the other hand. One says: "I was very nice to Mark when I called him from my friend's place and he answered. We'd arranged to go out that Saturday night but he hadn't called me to confirm. I thought he had the right to choose who he wanted to go out with and that I didn't have the right to protest because he hadn't picked me." Anne continues: "I tried to act normally. I was very polite and I asked him how he was, if he was very busy, and so on . . .

When I hung up I ran to the bathroom to vomit from how bad I felt."

Women my daughters' age have learned to want honesty in their daily life in the same measure as they fear the cruelty, both their own and others', of such a way of life. For them, truth may hurt but it is valuable in and of itself: as they are strong, they don't want to treat others nor to be treated with hypocritical courtesy or pious lies. But they don't know how to distinguish between truth-telling as a gesture of caring honesty and truth-telling as a way of renouncing responsibilities. Michelle says: "I told Andrew that I don't love him as much as he loves me. I think it's more honest if he knows, even though he might leave me." But she continues: "Now he knows. If he stays with me, that's his problem, not mine."

Some women like my daughters have learned since they were little the delicate pleasures of courtesy, but they also believe that such deference is only shown to the weak, to people who are dependent or inferior. They don't know when courtesies and friendliness in every day life are genuine and when they are demonstrations of weakness and submission.

They have learned since they were little that the truth is sacred, but they believe as well that the bad, those people only interested in caring for themselves, are capable of disguising themselves as good and of aggressing, attacking, maltreating or destroying the other in the name of honesty. They don't know when honest declarations are genuine and when they are simply dissimulated and hypocritical aggressions.

They have learned since they were little that he who believes in the love of power does not negotiate, but rather imposes himself; he does not ask, but rather takes what he wants; he does not thank, but rather demands.

But they have also learned that he who believes in the power of love does not negotiate, but rather gives in; he appreciates what is given, but makes no demands; he does not take, but rather gives the other what he wants.

Today, these women feel an enormous pleasure when they treat others and are themselves treated with courtesy, but they're never sure if this gesture (on their own or someone else's part) is an act of friendliness or of scorn, of respect or of humiliation, of sociability or of submission. They also feel an enormous pleasure when they take part in a true dialogue, but they're never sure if the words spoken are honest or malign, constructive or destructive, truthful or cruel.

Between the desire for courtesy and the fear of obsequiousness, between the desire for honesty and the fear of cruelty, how does one act? Their divided emotions lead them to argue with and to oppose themselves to their partners in order to feel that they love and are loved honestly, but also to seek consensus by eliminating difference, hiding disagreements, and so to feel that they love and are loved tactfully. They don't know whether they seek friendliness in their relationships as an effective way of living harmoniously or if they do so because of their own tendency towards servility and ultimately submission. Neither do they know whether they seek honesty in their relationships as an effective way of living respectfully and being respected or if they do so because of their own tendency towards an individualism that might end in violence.

Some women of my daughters' generation vacillate between violence and guilt, aggressions and repentance, obsequiousness and cruelty. They still don't know how, where, or in what way to look for a relationship that would be both, polite and honest, delicate and frank, at the same time and with the same intensity.

5. Between relaxation and exhilaration

Some women of my daughters' generation want both tranquility and exaltation from their relationships. They want both cozy predictable evenings and the constant possibility of self-transcendence. They reject the apathy and boredom that may be hidden within emotional calm as much as they fear the unforeseen inherent dangers of emotional exaltation. But they don't know how to distinguish between the sadness of an apathetic void and the calm of domestic satisfaction, between the attentions needed to explore new life paths and the tension required to participate in risky life games.

These women have learned early to enjoy the pleasures of a long tranquil evening at home, tasting their grandmothers' or mothers' poundcakes. And just the opposite: they have learned early to fear, reject, and hate silence, solitude, and the lack of stimuli of a house that contains merely the familiar routine. They surround themselves, they bask in, the attractions offered by theaters, restaurants, rowdy parties, the scent of airports, the music from all over introduced to them by globetrotting mothers or fathers. But they also drive themselves crazy by trying not to miss anything; they want to experience and enjoy everything all the time.

Some women like my daughters vacillate between the advantages of a domestic life and those of a worldly life. They ask themselves whether they prefer to care for a permanent household or to live—perhaps carefree—in transitory spaces; whether they need more the protection offered by known controllable scenarios or the liberty offered by surviving a series of ephemeral fleeting instants. They don't know whether to bore themselves with a husband who offers them a tranquilizing daily life or to divert themselves with a husband who offers them an angst-filled excitement composed of secrets and searches, deceptions and confessions, coquetries meant to flatter and then to trap, cat and mouse, mouse and cat, playing at the fascinating but unsatisfactory game of an eternally persecutory love.

They know well the advantages of urgency—adrenaline, hurdles to leap, constant changes, running so as not to be left behind—and they understand that in the professional world he wins who runs the fastest. But they also know well the advantages of pause—resting points, time to enjoy life as it happens, the satisfaction of not needing more and of being at peace—and they understand that in the emotional world he wins who knows how to live in the moment.

Today, some women of my daughters' generation seem to live on a constant emotional roller-coaster: they still don't know how, where, or in what way to look for a relationship that would let them enjoy both calm and excitement, tranquility and exaltation, the zenith and the nadir, night and day, the sated happiness of a fruitful autumn and the exuberant happiness of a blossoming spring.

6. Between outer-directedness and inner-directedness

Some women of my daughters' generation want both generosity and convenience in their emotional lives. So they reject the sacrifice required by silly forms of generosity as much as they fear the indifference required by selfish forms of looking out for one's own convenience.

They have learned how to enjoy the pleasure of emotional connection and communion felt by those who share their material and spiritual wealth generously. But they don't want to feel themselves taken advantage of by those who benefit from this generosity. They don't know how to distinguish between when they are being good and when stupid. They have also learned how to opt for situations and friendships that enrich them, that nourish them and that are convenient for them in their intellectual, emotional, socio-cultural progress. But they don't want to feel that they are vampires who cultivate only those relationships that benefit them: they don't want to take advantage of or to use anyone. They don't know how to distinguish between when they are being strong and when bad.

Natasha and Paula didn't accuse me of being stupid or selfish, but of being arbitrary. They never understood which criteria I used to determine when they had to be generous, to the extreme of giving away their toys, nor which belongings I felt were valuable and never to be even loaned to anyone. They chastised me for sometimes acting too generously and sometimes acting too selfishly. An example of the former: so generous I appeared stupid, according to my daughters, I paid for whatever classes they wanted without letting them decide which they really wanted to take. An example of the latter: so selfish I appeared incomprehensible, according to them, I refused to buy certain pieces of clothing if I myself didn't like them or didn't approve of their tastes. They didn't know if they should take advantage of my generosity and risk feeling Machiavellian or tolerate my selfishness and risk feeling submissive.

In their professional lives, some women of my daughters' age defend firmly their desires, needs, points of view, ideas and feelings: they think of themselves and of the other at once. They can be good by choosing what is best for the other because they are strong and know what is best for themselves.

But in their emotional lives they are not as successful. They have always heard that people who look out for themselves are speculators, bad people, people not interested in the community, people who do not respect social rules nor interest themselves in social ties. They have heard that those who do what is best for them do not love truth. They have learned that it's better to be generous and to make the lover happy, satisfying all his desires and meeting all his needs. They don't want to be selfish; they don't want to transform themselves into thieves or assailants of the emotions, benefiting from another's generosity or stupidity. They don't want to be more loved than loving. But neither do they want to be more loving than loved. They are not prepared to rob or let themselves be emotionally robbed.

They have learned that they must be hard and convex to penetrate and then to conquer the territories of power, but that they must be soft and concave to absorb the tenderness needed to win in the territories of love. And—today—they reject equally the ingenuity of those who give everything while expecting nothing in return and the cruelty of those who appropriate others' lives while giving nothing in return.

But how does one keep accounts and tabs in the emotional terrain? How pay the bills of love? When they show interest in the other without considering their own convenience, they suspect that the other will take advantage of them. They fear being stupid if they love too much. But they suspect that they are capable of taking advantage of the other when they consider whether or not to show their hands, emotionally speaking. They fear being manipulative if they speculate too much.

The fuzziness and lack of definition of their feelings converts these women into their own persecutors. They are dispersed in feeling, unable to prioritize, unable to sift through their contradictory feelings in order to arrive at some stable self-knowledge. They don't know if they gain more by giving generously of their love, without measuring, or by doling it out speculatively until even they do not know whether it is real or not. They don't know whether to be good, acting on their emotions without expecting any payback, or to be strong, hiding their thoughts until they're sure that the other is interested in them. In the process of maximizing this type of gain, love relationships mysteriously dissolve between their hands.

Some women of my daughters' generation are disconcerted. They wonder why, if they feel as good women do and think as strong women do, they still don't know how, where, or in what way to look for a relationship that is both generous towards and useful for both members of the couple.

7. Between pragmatism and idealism

Some women of my daughters' generation seek a relationship that assimilates utterly the ideal offered by the world of love while also knowing that reality marks the limits of the possible, as taught by the world of power. So they reject the ingenuity of romantic illusion as much as they fear the cynicism of romantic skepticism.

They learned to desire feelings that showed no doubt, an affirmation that life is only beautiful. At the same time, they learned to desire thoughts that showed no doubt, an affirmation that life is only ugly. They don't know which certainty is surer, which affirmation the more truthful; if he who loves is able to act or if he who is able to act, loves; if it's better to believe or to know; if life is a beautiful dream or death a horrible nightmare.

My daughters complained that I never let them believe in Santa Claus or in the Three Kings. They didn't like choosing their own presents, much less that I bought them useful things for their birthdays. They would have preferred to have the illusion of someone guessing what they wanted without their having to say anything. They wanted to believe in the magical existence of someone who would surprise them happily, someone capable of anticipating their needs. At the same time, they scorned their credulous friends; they considered their friends infantile for celebrating the commercialized rituals with which their parents placated them. My daughters preferred not to have to content themselves with the surprises they received, not to have to fake pleasure when they received gifts that struck them as inadequate. They appeared to think that nothing was better than realism as a way of feeling secure in life and safe from disagreeable surprises.

Some women of my daughters' generation continue not to know whether they prefer ideal or real relationships. They're romantics, but they feel contempt for themselves when they feel that they are too ingenuous, when they don't properly calculate the risks of a relationship. They're realists, but they scorn themselves when they are too cynical, too accepting of imperfections.

These women vacillate between the fear of robbing and the fear of being robbed, between the fear of exploiting and the fear of being exploited, between the fear of hunting and the fear of being hunted, between the fear of ingenuity and of cynicism, between the desire to believe and the need to know. They still don't know how, where, or in what way to look for a relationship that is idealistic and romantic and pragmatic and realist at once.

In learning the rules of power and the rules of love, these women developed abilities and needs so opposed to each other that they cancel one another out. They mastered contradictory languages and gestures, discovered thoughts and feelings that mutually destroy one another. They don't know what they feel, who they are, how to love or how they wish to be loved. They spin like maddened maddening tops to the rhythm of their contradictory desires—possessing and being possessed, manipulating and being manipulated, trusting and not trusting, believing and not believing, controlling and losing control, staying and leaving. They don't know how to define themselves emotionally: they see only fragments, bits of partial split loves, scattered tesserae that don't fit together into a mosaic of holistic ideal loves.

These women, some of them, stay in this whirling fragmented place: they are as multifaceted as they are confused, as fascinating as they are exasperating, radiant from energy as much as from desperation, as full of hope as of disillusion, trapped between the ideology of the power of love, that requires them to love as if they were only good, and the ideology of the love of power, that requires them to love as if they were only strong.

6

EPIDEMIC OF AMOROUS MISTRUST

Michelle, an American young woman born and raised amidst a traditional Bostonian family, enjoys an undoubtedly professional success in a prestigious New York law firm. Interested in meeting a life partner, she embarks on her romantic search with the same tenacity, the same rigor, the same discipline and strength with which she pursues her career. Nevertheless, the results of her work are not as successful in her love life as they are in her professional life.

She tells of her relationship with Juan, a Colombian colleague who comes from as traditional and successful a family as hers and who works in a equally prestigious law firm: "I think my professional success is based on how much I feel rejected by men. I have to prove that I'm someone. But all the honors I receive do nothing to take away this horrible feeling of being less than other people because I'm single. I feel that I have a little of everything but nothing of anything real when I'm rejected again and again by these players. I don't know how to play with them. I'm worse since my sister had her baby. On Sunday I slept with Juan without wanting to, because after six months of seeing each other almost every night he still hasn't told me that he loves me, I felt masculine, as if my sexuality had been 'caught' from men's sexuality, as if having sex were a sport in which you can't show any feeling that might compromise the performance, another activity in daily urban life. Worse, the next day I couldn't work, hoping that he would call me; I couldn't stop looking at the phone. I can't stand how cruel he is to me. Monday night I dreamt that a man whose face I couldn't see was holding me peacefully and tenderly."

I ask her: "If he's so cruel, why do you stay with him?"

She answers: "Well, the truth is that we hadn't made arrangements for him to call me, it's that I wanted to control him because I can't stand not knowing what he's doing or where he is when we're not together. I wanted him to call me, even though I knew we would both be very busy that week and wouldn't be able to see each other."

I ask her: "Why didn't you ask him to call you?"

She answers: "Because I didn't want him to say what he always says, which is that it's always me asking him for something. Now I think I won't return his call when he does call. But I'm scared that then I'll be sorry, and if he doesn't insist and calls me out of the blue I'll feel worse."

Some women of my daughters' generation want the advantages of one model of love while fearing the concurrent disadvantages. They want to revel in emotional dependence, in the sensation of being connected to someone who cares for them, decides for them, and thinks for them as much as they fear losing their emotional independence and the liberty of making their own decisions. They want to revel in the heat of a *we* as much as they fear losing the energetic affirmation of an *I*. They want to bask in the calm of a stable, polite, generous and idealistic relationship as much as they fear losing the advantages of relationships that are new, exciting, convenient and pragmatic.

They wish to dedicate themselves passionately to their professions as much as they fear feeling that they are bad mothers or bad spouses if they do so. They want to dedicate themselves to the care of their children and their homes but they fear feeling stupid or being relegated to oblivion if they do so. Georgina, an architect who has stopped pursuing her profession while she cares for her young children, becomes angry when her husband says, socially, "my wife takes care of the kids." She asks him: "Have you forgotten that I'm a professional?" But she also becomes angry if he says, "my wife's an architect." She says: "You're embarrassed that your wife doesn't work, it strikes you as nothing that I'm taking care of the kids and house." Women like her feel that they want to be honest and not to fall back on emotional manipulation in order to capture men's attention. But when they act in this way they run the risk of being accused of not being seductive or womanly enough. They feel that they want to be sensitive, spontaneous and intuitive. But when they act in this way they run the risk of being accused of being irrational, temperamental or out of control. They feel that they want to be determined and ambitious. But when they act in this way they run the risk of being considered too aggressive and materialistic. They want to be decisive but are accused of being authoritarian; they want to be proactive but are accused of being invasive. They want to defend mutual respect but they know when they act in this way, that they run the risk of coming face to face with a lack of such respect.

Bill, a young Jewish American man very successful in the art world, writes to Andrea: "I feel deeply ashamed of the way I yelled at you last night. I ask your pardon for having treated you as if I were an insensitive and bad person. This e-mail isn't a justification, but a way of trying to understand why I get so violent when you won't accept my compliments. When I told you how special you are to me, and how much I wanted our relationship to grow and for us to grow together, you answered with a long silence. When I asked what you were thinking of, you told me that you were preoccupied by work. I felt as if you had slapped me. I don't want a woman who doesn't have her own life but I also don't want one who won't let me into her life. I've acted in this way in other relationships but I don't want that with you. I hate that you don't trust me and now I see that getting angry makes you distance yourself from me which is exactly what I don't want."

But a few weeks later, Bill tells a friend: "I don't know if I'm so in love with Andrea. Sometimes she seems like an unbearable weight, hysterical. But if I show any doubts it's worse: she leaves me that minute. And I'm not prepared for her to decide when the relationship is over. At least I want her to realize that she's also got something to lose if we break up."

Juan, the man Michelle slept with reluctantly, says: "Michelle is perfect. She's beautiful, intelligent, sensitive and independent. I'm sure my mother would love her. I don't know why I don't tell her I love her. I can't be tender with her. I think I don't want her to love me because I'm scared of disillusioning her. I don't feel capable of loving her as she deserves. I don't like treating women as if they're disposable, playthings I get rid of when I've used them up, but I can't help it. I need them very much. I can't live without a woman's love. I'm scared of ending up with someone who wants to get married but don't love me for myself, with someone who catches me with my guard down and traps me without my even realizing."

Some men of my daughters' generation don't know how to act in the world of love. They know the advantages of being sensitive, spiritual, democratic and good receivers of the needs, opinions and desires of others. But they also know the disadvantages of being idealistic, living in the air, showing themselves as overly innocent. They grew up learning that it was to their benefit to be determined and firm in their convictions in order to distinguish themselves from overly soft men, but also that they shouldn't be macho or prepotent. They grew up learning to admire, love and respect women but also fearing to reveal themselves as fools should they be ensnared by feminine wiles.

Like women of their generation, they fear being weak if they are good and they fear being bad if they are strong.

Michelle and Juan and Andrea and Bill become angry when they feel they've been treated as weak by their partners, when they feel humiliated, maltreated or scorned. But they also suffer anguish when they feel that they are bad, when they feel that they humiliate, maltreat or scorn the other.

Women and men of my daughters' generation who learned the advantages of both the power of love and the love of power doubt their own emotions. They are strong but wish not to be bad, they are good but wish not to be weak. But they don't know how to be strong without being bad, or how to be good without being weak. They live in a state of constant emotional contradiction: if they gain liberty, they feel that they lose security; if they gain security, they feel that they've lost liberty.

They don't want to be like their parents: they don't want to have only one piece of a dichotomous emotional world. They don't want to live emotionally declawed as they have seen their parents do. They aspire to the enjoyment of the advantages of both ideologies of love while they hope to avoid the disadvantages of each. But they don't know of what consists a relationship that is both strong and good. They want everything but fear being left with nothing: they doubt their own feelings and those of others.

They do not know how to choose. They do not know how to prioritize their desires. They don't know which way of being, which relationship, which approach to love, would bring them more happiness in life. They don't know what they want or why they are wanted; neither the men nor the women know what they offer or what they ask in a relationship. They don't know if they should look for someone to marry or someone to pursue, someone to enjoy tenderly or to have passionately, someone with whom to build a stable life and family or someone with whom to continue expanding their individual liberties.

When they aspire to all the advantages and none of the disadvantages of the two ideologies of love, these women and men discover that they have no signposts: they believe in everything as much as they doubt everything. In such a state, certainty cannot exist.

They alternate between surprising behaviors. Sometimes they exercise an almost skeptical lucidity and severity in their relationships, a warrior's determination in their emotional demands. Their looks and their comments at such times are scary. But at other times they show an almost ingenuous idealism and fragility, a humble insecurity in their emotional demands. Their looks and comments at such time cause pain. It's hard to understand whether their difficulties come from a profound devaluation of themselves or from a shocking pride, from extreme dependence or exaggerated independence.

In their relationships, both men and women suffer. They suffer as much from being victims as from being victors, as much from feeling weak and humiliated as from feeling cruel and bad. They don't know how to classify what they feel. They don't know what name, what form, what face to give to the love they are seeking. They don't know how to keep accounts of their romantic victories and losses.

Sometimes they see themselves as masochists, insensitive, perpetually unsatisfied. They believe that they love too much or too little, never enough, adequately, the right amount.

But these are not the correct diagnoses. These men and women suffer because both are, at once, too mistrusting and too credulous.

They mistrust: they know that to progress in life one must be free, must not need anything from anyone, must never lose one's head or let emotions interfere with one's ambition. But they also believe: they know that there is no pleasure greater than to find oneself safe in someone else's arms, no liberty greater than to declare oneself, in the words of Octavio Paz, "a slave of the beloved." They mistrust: they know that victories in the world of power augment when one takes advantage of the doubts, mistakes and weaknesses of the other players who are, by definition, enemies to be annulled or disappeared. But they also believe: they know that victories in the world of love augment when one takes into account only the virtues and merits of the loved one. They don't know how to do as they like, how to be strong and mistrusting, while at the same time doing what the other wants, being good and trusting.

Strange love, which defines as manipulation honest and careful outreach, as hypocrisy efforts against skepticism, as cowardice gestures of friendliness. Strange love, which makes losers of winners and winners of losers. And strange this love of power that condemns to mistrust in order to protect against the dangers of this power of love that condemns to belief.

To mistrust while seeking trust. To love while trying not to love. Not to love while trying to love. Such are the titles of the amorous dances of these women and men, who so fear being bad that they make themselves weak, who so fear being weak that they make themselves bad; who so seek absolute perfection that they mutually infect one another with romantic mistrust. These complex people recognize each other better than they understand each other. They attract each other more than they care to admit. They intuit that the other is emotionally rare, different, perhaps unique. They intuit that the other is full of strength and loyalty, but they don't manage to delve in enough to know whether they've found a wonder or a danger, a difference that is extraordinarily beautiful and nurturing or extraordinarily malignant and ugly. These traits do not manifest themselves as they did in past generations: strength and weakness, goodness and badness are different from what they were. And so men and women today do not understand what they see or know how to show what they want the other to see. And, faced with each successive encounter, they become more and more disconcerted, more and more fearful and mistrusting.

In love relationships, some men and women do not know.

Strong women (and men) who don't want to be bad do not know, but they refuse to resolve this not-knowing with the tools of the workplace: they refuse to think.

They blame their difficulties on the fact that they think too much: they believe that their intelligence prevents them from feeling as they should. They believe that if they are strong they are not good; that if they do as they please they are Machiavellian; that if they don't give in to their feelings without thinking, they do not love enough. And, in a supreme act of love of Love, they decide not to think about their relationships. Invoking the miracle of an ideal encounter, they are going to be good by only feeling.

They will neither see nor understand that which they do not like in their men or in themselves. They are going to believe. Arbitrarily, with no information except their desires, they convince themselves that they love and are loved. They base these decisions in feelings that cannot be thought over or through. They decide to be optimistic and not to worry about the consequences of a poorly taken romantic decision because they fear destroying through pessimism the scant romantic possibilities that seem to exist for women such as them.

Desperate to combat their inner cynicism, they lop off a vital part of themselves and dedicate themselves to feeling. They affirm that a thought-over love is not love.

Strong women who don't want to be bad promise themselves that, if they put down the powerful arm of intelligence, the capacity to think through and understand what is happening in the romantic game, they will stop doubting. They try to convince themselves that love is a question of skin or of chemistry, and that having butterflies in the stomach is all one needs to know if one has found true love. They believe that if they need to make an effort to understand what causes their attraction, or what kind of encounter they are part of, or what consequences might follow from the encounter, then what they have found is not love. They affirm that love is magical; anything else is not love.

They believe that if they ask questions, if they confide emotional information in the other and evaluate what the other has confided in them, if they try to discover whether the offered embrace is trustworthy and safe, then the attraction of the mystery will disappear along with the desire to conquer. They believe that love vanishes if it transforms itself into a convenience. These women affirm that love is not convenient.

If they win using their abilities as strong women, evaluating their partners and themselves with the precision of which they are capable, they suspect themselves of being bad. As such, they lose points in the world of love. They decide, thus, that if they want to feel they must not look for information or try to understand their or their partners' feelings or lose time in dialogue or look out for themselves. They decide that the best proof of true love is to give oneself over without considering risks, to let oneself go in a voluntary loss of control. They trust that, if they let themselves go, they will reach the epiphany of a total and complete embrace. They affirm the cautious love is not the real thing.

To fall in love as they wish—irrationally, passionately, entirely—they shut out reality. The truth will be that which they feel without seeing, without looking, without thinking, without understanding. Love must combine in a strange and impassioned formula suspicions and credulities, mistrust and ingenuity. They affirm that realistic love is not the real thing.

For fear of being bad, they make themselves weak. By choice they annul their intelligence and transform themselves into silly girls without the capacity to make discernments. They reject or do not allow themselves to know any datum that could lead them to mistrust. They insist on giving the other the benefit of the doubt because they claim this benefit for themselves. They act as if love's only form is that of *A Midsummer Night's Dream*: a spell, an enchantment, a flight of fancy.

Good men (and women) who do not want to be weak do not know how to act in their relationships, but they refuse to solve this not-knowing with the tools of the workplace: they refuse to feel.

They believe that their difficulties come from the fact that they feel too much: they believe that their sensibility prevents them from thinking as they should. They believe that if they are good they are not strong; if they do what the other wants they are stupid; if they give in to their feelings without reason, they love too much. And, in a supreme act of love of power, they decide not to feel in their relationships. They are going to only think, in order to be strong and to protect themselves from the risks of traitorous encounters and divided loves.

They decide to shut up within themselves any feelings that 'soften' them or that expose them to the danger of being trapped where, when, and by whom they do not wish to be.

For fear of disappearing in the romantic encounter, they try to forget that they feel, what they feel and how they feel. Arbitrarily, with no information other than their fears, they convince themselves that they neither love nor are loved. They base these decisions in thoughts that cannot be felt. They decide to be skeptics and not to believe in any possibility of love. In a desperate attempt at protection, they refuse any hint of optimism. They try to convince themselves that love is an old wives' tale in which the witches win.

The women (and men) who believe and the men (and women) who mistrust suppose that they know the truth, but both un-thought feelings and un-felt thoughts constitute partial truths. Neither the men nor the women notice that both credulity and mistrust are feelings that determine attitudes and set courses of conduct as if their conclusions were based on certain rational information. Both the credulous and the mistrusting arrange that the eyes see what the heart feels.

Both the women and men who decide not to think and those who decide not to feel circulate constantly between mistrust and credulity, between idealization and disillusion. Both seek a relationship that gives sustenance, but both create relationships that provoke suffering and threats that cause jealousy and fears of abandonment. Both believe that love, if it's to be considered available, appropriates the life and the identity of the lover.

When the defensive strategies of women and men who are strong but don't want to be bad meet, the painful mis-encounters between them are aggravated. Both return to the world of love more fragile, thinking that they are stronger: the women abandon the teachings of power; the men abandon the teachings of love. As a result, both move in the rhythms marked by the mistrusts and credulities of those who refuse to think about love. As a sign of their love for the other, they do not take any preventative measures. They do not take care of themselves. So as not to appear mistrusting they act credulous. The lack of care exposes them to risk: they feel pitied, attacked, badly loved: they take exaggerated defensive measures that the other sees as a declaration of war. So as not to appear credulous they mistrust.

This romantic choreography begins with an encounter: they look at each other, they sniff at each other; they recognize each other. They suspect that they have something in common and they are right. Only a complex man can understand the emotional complexities of a complex woman and vice-versa. But both either fear appearing bad or weak, or of discovering that their partner is bad or weak. They fear the possibility of being more interested in the other than the other is in them, and so of running the risk of appearing weak, vulnerable and dependent. But they also fear the opposing possibility: that of being less interested in the other than the other is in them and so of running the risk of appearing bad, cynical or indifferent. Both fear rejecting as much as being rejected. To protect themselves, they don't show what they feel. They don't look each other in the face, they don't explore intimacy.

The dance continues with a chaotic sequence of miss-encounters and misunderstandings, mistrusting and credulities. No one wants to take the first step, no one wants to show the confusion of his emotions, no one wants to show himself as bad or feel himself to be weak, as they remember how their parents, in a constant game of up and down, push and pull, played. They only reveal one of their parts: if they want to let themselves be conquered, they speak of their goodness; if they want to conquer, they speak of their strengths. They don't discover themselves fully, nor do they discover the other fully, because in the field of love they do not know how to be both strong and good at once.

In this masked dance of men and women who don't show themselves as they are because they don't know who they are, no one becomes acquainted with anyone else. They keep moving without knowing whether their dance partners are interested in them, without letting the partners know of their own interests. No one asks anything, no one confides anything; no one gives clear signs either of interest or of lack of interest. The dance involves a continual effort to discover the other without revealing oneself. It is a dance of a love that is blind, deaf and dumb.

When one of the dancers takes a real step amidst all this mistrusting and hiding, the partner—who does not know how to read the new movement—reacts without stopping to consider whether what he feels corresponds with reality. He does not think: he acts. If he feels attacked, he attacks; if he feels abandoned, he abandons. The one who receives this reaction to an action that was not meant as an aggression reacts in turn without stopping to consider whether the other misinterpreted his original gesture. Seeing himself attacked, he attacks. Seeing himself abandoned, he abandons. And so an escalation of intentional violence begins to develop, originating in a vicious circle of misunderstandings.

As the Greek tragedies show, some disastrous endings are the result of misunderstandings, of taking friends for enemies, declarations of peace as declarations of war. The moral of these magisterial works is that if we are determined to fight we can convince ourselves that even the most explicit show of love is a threat against which we must defend ourselves. Could this series of romantic miss-encounters have been prevented? Could some of these tragic errors have been avoided? He who took the first step soon forgets what he felt in that moment. Now both feel, justly, invaded by rage or sadness. Both feel truly attacked or abandoned. Now, both are truly trapped in a climate of confrontation, mistrust and war. And each tries to convince himself that he is the weak one in the couple, that the other is bad.

But the worm of doubt torments both: in spite of the fact that both feel unjustly attacked and tell their family and friends that it is all the other's fault, they ask themselves: Did I want to attack or abandon myself, did I provoke this? Each fears having been the bad one, the one who took advantage of the other's weakness.

Both keep dancing for fear of confirming, once again, that they've been wrong: either they were too bad and didn't know how to love or they were too weak and didn't know how to make themselves loved. When they think they've been bad, they begin to move as if they were weak, in order to be forgiven by the supposedly good one. But this confession of guilt doesn't work: neither one feels either as bad or as weak as he claims. Both know themselves and the other to be strong and good, but they lack a code that would let them understand these odd kinds of goodness and strength.

Women and men who don't know how to read their own feelings cannot read those of others. So they run the risk of feeling unjustly attacked in response to gestures they've made in an effort to become closer to the beloved, if this latter misinterprets the gesture as a declaration of war. And they run the risk of feeling loved without merit if they interpret as strong committed declarations of love what the other meant only as a friendly advance. The suspicion of an unjust attack or an unmerited affection augments their mistrust of themselves and of their partners, and with the suspicion comes also an increase in the difficulties of creating the longed-for encounter. The dance of mistrust and credulity ends in a frenetic and inevitable rhythm of amorous skepticism.

These women and men ignore the fact that romantic miss-encounters happen because they forget that, by definition, dancing in couple requires two people. They leap from the rhythm of mistrust, in which they attack or abandon in order to protect themselves from lack of love, to the rhythm of credulity, in which they submit or run risks in order to encourage love. But they never engage in dialogue. It does not occur to them to seek complicities with the other or to learn how to dance with the other. It does not occur to them that, if they want to know, the first step is recognizing that they don't know and asking.

Those who mistrust don't know if they are just or unjust, if they defend themselves or attack. When these people feel bad for not trusting, they castigate themselves and demand from themselves more credulity, more ingenuity; more weakness. When they feel too weak, they become scared, they harden themselves and they attack; when they feel too strong they fear not knowing how to love and they stop thinking. This vicious circle feeds the contagious system of amorous mistrust.

The epidemic spreads most rapidly among those who best know how to play the contradictory games of power and love. The mistrust protects from credulity which protects from cynicism which protects from ingenuity which protects from mistrust. But both cynicism and credulity prevent one from seeing what the dance partner is seeking in the encounter. Both defensive strategies work as impenetrable armor that makes true intimacy impossible. Both strategies hide fears, weaknesses and insecurities, but also work as obfuscator signals for both partners, who are converted at once into hunters and hunted, predators and prey. Everyone loses in this way of loving: the credulous prey loses, because he feels weak; the mistrusting predator, because he feels bad.

How to ensure that competition does not destroy love? How to avoid humiliating and being humiliated, submitting or making others submit, maltreating or being maltreated? How do two strong people relate without mutually destroying each other? How do two good people relate without mutually boring each other? How does one live in a constant state of alertness, doing as one likes, and at the same time, live in a constant state of passion, doing what the other likes? How does one engage while still protecting oneself? How does one protect oneself while still engaging? How can one be, at once, both lover-hunter and beloved-hunted, desiring subject and desired object? No one knows. But the difficulties grow because each one thinks the other knows and refuses to tell. And if the response, when it comes, is a confession of ignorance and a desire to learn together, they are not satisfied. They have reached the point at which possible love does not strike them as love, precisely because it is possible.

A vast panorama of offers complicates the lack of criteria for choosing a way of living or of loving. They may live alone, with others, in homosexual or traditional or non-traditional heterosexual couples. They may decide not to have children or to adopt or to be single parents or to share parenting responsibilities with biological parents. In every option, they wonder constantly if they gain more by being strong and powerful or good and loving, by strengthening themselves and doing what they want or by resting and doing what the other wants. Thoughts and feelings tumble around and around, making them dizzy; making them want to stop and disembark from the kaleidoscopic carousel of relationships.

7

CHOREOGRAPHIES OF LOVE

In May 1998, Andrea received an e-mail from Vanessa, inviting her to participate in the creation of a *Women's Committee against Sons of Bitches*. The e-mail informed her about the group's first meeting that was to take place in one of her favorite restaurants in New York, a place frequented by young banking and financial types like her. The main discussion points included:

"1. How to ensure that men's blows don't hurt.
2. How to slap their snouts to punish them without hurting yourself.
3. How to live with the other sex without compromising yourself emotionally.
4. How to use and abuse men in order to be happy."

Continuing, the invitation emphasized that 'the urgency of the topic' required 'enthusiastic participation' and asked people to confirm whether or not they would be attending.

Vanessa's invitation did not surprise Andrea. The latter is also enraged at men, also speaks badly about them, also believes that men neither understand women nor embrace them properly. But unlike her friend and colleague from work, a young female economist from Brazil who also chose Manhattan as her permanent place of residence and who proudly declares herself strong and bad, Andrea does not want to triumph over men, or make them disappear from her life, or transform them into harmless puppies.

Vanessa and other women like her don't doubt: they are convinced that, in life, the fittest survive. When they affirm that, in romantic relationships with the opposite sex, the strong is in a better position than the weak, they base their ideas in evolutionary law. True hunters, they want to be the fittest in the game of love and they are prepared to survive at any cost. They know that they must be very strong if they want to deploy efficiently the principles of power. They know that if they want to do as they like they can't let emotions interfere with their objectives, as emotional ties are dangerous; they know that they must always be on guard, waiting for the best moment to quarry their prey and to defend themselves against other hunters. If the cost of getting what they want is to be considered bad, they are prepared to pay it with interest: the pleasure of vengeance merits it.

Women like Vanessa consider themselves the proud heirs of those women who struggled for the right to enjoy the same liberties as those enjoyed by strong men. In the name of weak women who were abandoned, humiliated, and betrayed by bad men, these women assume with dignity the heroic role of bad women.

For them, the world is divided into the strong and the weak. They believe that all people, including those who seem good, seek their own advantage. Those who do what the other wants don't do so out of altruism but because they cannot do otherwise: they must make the other (the strong) need them. It's a good way of ensuring one's own protection, a good survival strategy for those with limited resources (emotional, material, social, intellectual or abilities to stand their own desire).

They aspire not to need anyone and to live an independent life, free of any submission to outside wills or desires; they know that, as strong women, they will be considered bad, selfish, insensitive and unloving. They know that they will be treated as dangerous people, as the cause of all worldly evil. Rather than explain that such is not the case, they prefer to declare themselves bad women. They know that, in any case, no one will believe their protestations to the contrary. Weak people prefer not to know that the strong also lack, suffer, need. "Since they already accuse me of being the most bad, I'll be the worst," is the *lemma* with which they defend themselves from these injustices.

In relationships, these women try to avoid being men's victims by acting like the victors. They don't realize that, by defending themselves in this way from the dangers of ingenuity, weakness and credulity, they perpetuate the dangers of cynicism, badness and mistrust.

There is always a bad man lurking on their emotional horizons: everyone can be a thief who wants to take advantage of them. They think: "Best to cure oneself of the temptation to be stupidly generous," and, in defense of emotional liberty, they fight with teeth and nails. Women who adhere to the rules of power always find some reason to criticize and to doubt. They consider dangerous, deceitful or thieving even men from whom they receive care. They protect themselves so fiercely from the dangers of being weakened by love that they end up hiding from themselves their own desires to love. Tenderness—their own or another's—and letting oneself be swayed by loving emotions sets off in them an intolerable sensation of vulnerability: they are invaded by an uncontrollable fear of losing control of their emotions or of another losing such control. Strong women who proudly declare themselves bad prefer to choose weak men who are so interested in being or being considered good that they will do what the other wants without demanding reciprocity. This relationship model maintains the choreography of relationships in my grandparents' time: in this case, the roles have been inverted, and here the man cares for the woman how and when it is convenient for her. The weak man must understand what he has to do and how to obey orders without taking the initiative, including his own ideas, speaking in his own voice or giving importance to his own needs when making decisions that affect both. Strong women who don't fear being bad don't require that their men think. The women know how to think as the men do, or better.

The strong woman of my daughters' age usually is as arbitrary in the use of her economic power as was my grandfather with his wife, and, like him, the strong woman is subject to the emotional manipulations of the weak one, who does what she wants in order for her to do what he wants. But these men and women are usually happy with each other: each one, as an individual, obtains what is useful for him or her. She obtains total control and responsibility; he obtains freedom from both.

In relationships that respect the competitive rules of the world of power, a *we* does not exist and neither does dialogue. One hears only arid monologues and eloquent declarations of principles beginning always with the word *I*. Faced with a strong man, the monologue of the strong woman stops before it starts, and the voice of the supposed receiver is barely heard either, as his monologues also always begin with *I*.

Strong bad women fear being conquered, becoming a prisoner of their own entrapping webs and transforming themselves into contemptible (and feminine) trophies of a hunter better than they, so much that they will only enter into relationships with strong men if these men are younger than they are.

They let themselves be used by these young men, avid little eagles interested in learning all that the women can teach them, while the women also use the men: with them, they feel potent, powerful and highly sexed. But they never forget that relationships must offer mutual utility and that it's best to end them before too long, so that all remain free to go in search of a better opportunity.

They leave the game as soon as they begin to suspect that they will be left for or exchanged for other women. If they let themselves be carried away by jealousy and try to keep the men, they will have lost: this jealousy is the first sign that they are no longer in control, they are no longer the strongest; they are no longer hunters. They have become what they most despise: contemptible prey. They feel sick: they are in love.

Strong bad women do not doubt: they are convinced that one must not connect to another. Falling in love is a dangerous illness.

Andrea surprised herself with her own response to Vanessa's e-mail. She replied: "I hope you don't accuse me of being a traitor. I will attend the meeting but I want to change the premise. I propose that we try to understand:

1. How to relate to men who are scared of forming ties to strong women like us.
2. How not to pity them so that they won't pity us.
3. How to love them and how to learn how to receive their love."

Andrea is strong but she does not wish to be bad. Unlike Vanessa, she does not believe that all people are bad, nor that all men are dangerous enemies of women, nor that incomprehension between the sexes is caused by an inevitable definite essence. Andrea does not want to be less than a man but neither does she want to be like a man. She wishes to think neither against nor like a man; she wishes to think with him. But she does not know how.

As a girl, she used to say that when she was grown up and had kids she wouldn't be able to take them to school because she would be riding around on her motorbike, and that her mother, the future grandmother, would have to look after the children. As an adolescent, she had a recurrent dream in which she rode a powerful motorcycle past her school friends' favorite crushes, while looking past the boys haughtily. These dreams usually ended badly. At the start she felt happy because she went by without even looking at them, thus showing that she didn't need them like her stupid girlfriends. But when she looked back to see how they were reacting to her affront, she saw that she was different from them and scraped her legs against a wall and fell. She awoke invaded by a feeling of humiliation because her female body didn't let her ride a bike as if she were a man.

Andrea seems to inhabit the same emotional terrain as Vanessa, but Vanessa thinks of Andrea as a complacent man-pleasing traitor.

Andrea cannot defend herself against men as her friend proposes. She does not resolve her difficulties by breaking off a part of herself, by remaining in a world of divided love. She hopes to find a love that is both strong and good.

And so she accepts with more hope and with more ingenuity than Vanessa the embrace of strong men who seem interested in her. She dares to fall in love, to believe in him, not to protect herself from him. Andrea and other women like her know that the world orders itself according to the rules of power but they also hope for the miracles promised by the rules of love. When they discover that the men who interest them are strong but also bad, it is already too late. They have already been imprisoned in love's cage, humiliated, offended, weak, doing what the other wants. They have already transformed themselves into victims of men's badness. And they already feel alone, abandoned, famished for love.

If other men, moved by their sad gazes, offer them their embrace, these women accept and let themselves be carried off, newly hopeful. Perhaps this will be the longed-for encounter. But their hope lasts only a moment, only until they remember that these men too are strong and obey the rules of power, even if they are trying to be good and to live in a way commanded by the rules of love.

Let us imagine these encounters. In the first steps of this choreography, the man leads and the woman—so suffocated, weighed down, brutalized by the disasters that were her past relationships that she does not even ask herself what being bad or good means—rests. Until she recovers her own strength—and in this moment, everything changes. She returns abruptly to an erect posture, she frees herself from the embrace that has begun to feel claustrophobic, she looks at herself, she looks at him, she asks herself: "What am I doing here? What is this man doing here?"

When she understands that she feels better thanks to the affectionate care of this weak man—weak because he must be almost stupid to have fallen in love with her without noticing that she can be bad, and so it is not sufficient that he is good—she tries to pay him back or to compensate him. She tries to correct him and to show him how and where to put his feet, his hands, his head: she shows him how he should live, work, behave, think and feel in order to win in the world of power. She nags, thinking that she knows better than he what is good for him; she criticizes, thinking to educate him; she puts him down, thinking to push him to fulfill his ambition. He thanks her for her lessons but does not employ what she has taught him. Maybe because he doesn't want more power, maybe because he's not rapid enough to learn the rhythm that she imposes, maybe because he truly is weak.

She takes the next step: she holds herself back, startled by her own violence. If he's good, he offers her again his compassionate embrace. But this only makes her feel guiltier because she knows she can't help but waste what he gives her. They recommence the dance in a rhythm of tender friendship, a cadence that maintains itself until she, more enraged all the time at the unjustified and exaggerated friendliness of her partner, decided that they cannot keep dancing together: she doesn't tolerate feeling that she is bad and, even though she tries to avoid this, her rhythms will always be faster and her sights set higher than his. It's true that this man doesn't act as if he were a dangerous eagle ready to take advantage of an innocent dove. But she, until now a siren delighted with her role, begins to think that she is like an octopus capable of entrapping him, of killing him in a sticky asphyxiating embrace. She doesn't know who scares her more, herself or him. She decides to leave him; she thinks that he should accept that she needs liberty more than she needs his embrace.

Freed from love's ballast—the constant close presence of a man whose care strikes her as a demand for care, whose love is to her a demand for love—she can continue on her path and fly as high as she wants without worrying about the destiny of a weak person.

When they overcome their depression or fear and recover their desires, these women can't escape their curiosity towards the unknown, their ambition for broader horizons, their anxiety to live in a full exciting world, their want of a passion not found in the arms of these men. The men notice. They admire the women's ability to run around taking care of work, of children, of their family and friends, of the gym, of cultural activities. But they also fear these out of control creatures who are so demanding and impatient, who argue all the time about nothing. Unlike women such as Vanessa, who don't fear being bad or selfish, these women are not content to feel loved. They also want to be generous and to love. Strong women who want to be good cannot stand feeling disqualified to love by conformist men who, ingenuously, want everyone to be happy.

Good weak men make these women feel that they are so bad (more ambitious than they themselves suspect), so cruel (less ingenuous than they seem), and so unfriendly (more critical than they at first appear), that these (emotionally confused) women prefer to avoid their embraces. But they make the mistake of accepting, when they are tired of their solitary flights or when someone has hurt them. These women don't know how to defend themselves from strong bad men either; with them, women like Andrea feel unbearably humiliated, intolerably weak. Women like Andrea test the embrace of strong men until they discover that the men are also bad, and then return to the comforts of good men, that last until they discover that these men are not only good but also weak . . .

Why do the dances between weak good men and strong good women end badly? Because the women doubt: they believe that all human relationships are based in convenience or manipulative strategies, while also believing that solidarity, understanding and empathy exist. The problem is that they don't know when they are being strong and when malignant, when they are being good and when inconsistent.

Unlike Vanessa, women like Andrea don't abandon the romantic hope of one day meeting a complete man, a man who wants to be both strong and good. They are prepared to do a little less of what they want and a little more of what he wants. But they don't know how to do this without feeling 'femininely' weak.

And their relationships with men like themselves—strong men who don't want to be bad, men who want to be good without being weak—end with both parties infected by mistrust.

At a major gala celebrating the year 2000, a man noted that the husband of one of the guests was much thinner and more elegant than previously. Even though the comment had not been directed to her, Catherine, a young architect who had graduated with honors and who only had practiced her profession for some months before getting married, said: "Of course, I've got him well taken care of." A perfect synthesis of the self-definition of women who live successfully in the world of love: victorious protagonists on whom the fact of playing their role well confers social standing and legitimacy. And here the goodness is doubly strong: the comment refers to an increase in health, which varies with the quality of loving care as opposed to with amounts of money, a subject for those who are strong and bad. Catherine is convinced of being good and does not fear feeling weak: she sustains the principles of the power of love. She does not doubt: she holds firmly to the idea of emotional security. She believes in dependence, in the permanence of repeated rituals, in romantic traditions.

She does not question her own potency: she's convinced that all human relations, including those most infused by power, obey the rules of love. She believes that even in the most malignant soul there resides, hidden, fearful, a bit of goodness.

Women like Catherine are proud heirs of those women who sacrificed their personal lives in defense of the sanctity of hearth and home; they are the origins and centers of emotional life; they are priestesses of love. They are convinced that all human actions, even including the murder, domination or digestion of another, are motivated by the desire to love or to make oneself loved.

They believe that those who love most are those who most sacrifice themselves and transform themselves into slaves of their loved ones. In transforming men into their absolute rulers, these women make their men absolutely responsible for them. The men must answer for the quality of these women's lives, including their economic well-being and emotional satisfaction. The rule of love awards women who renounce protagonism: it protects them from the risk of making a bad personal decision.

As they demonstrate time and again, they act when they are swayed by their emotions and value only those who don't calculate the results or risks of their romantic acts. They are extremely jealous, with the goal of guarding their property. They feel themselves to be the true defenders of traditional family values, those that perpetuate the family in spite of the threatening consequences of the emotional progress of independent women. They never think that their care might be a form of possessive control nor that their self-abnegating manner of privileging their husbands' and children's activities over their own might be a way of avoiding criticisms, competition or conflict.

"I shall not let my husband ruin my marriage," says Susanita, a character in the Argentine comic strip *Mafalda*. Women like Catherine never mistrust; in particular, they never mistrust themselves.

They transmit such a strong feeling of trust and confidence in themselves and in all of humanity, they believe so much in themselves, that they infect others with happiness and hope—beliefs that life is always beautiful, endings always happy, pots of gold wait at the end of every rainbow. Even the most cynical of men is tempted by this romantic nourishment. It's very agreeable to let oneself be convinced by these women, who believe that bad people are merely lost sheep who have not been given sufficient love. These women look for, and make themselves found by, bad men who aspire to be reformed. The women feel for both partners; the men don't need to feel.

Some of these lost bad men honestly want to be good and think that entering the idyllic world of the rule of love will cure their wounds, cleanse them of their sins. Others are interested only in gaining a professional competitive advantage via their love life: they are strong, but they know that they would be more attractive and better conquerors in the economic jungle if they appeared to be good. They prefer to keep separate power and love, outside and inside, work and home, passion and tenderness. They and their good women believe that dividing the worlds of power and love favors the establishment of lasting relationships. These men and women are happy together as long as each member of the couple believes that he is doing what the other wants.

In this type of choreography, gains amass quickly because there exists only a *we*. Each member of the couple acts as if he were simply an extension of the other. "My wife knows/has/can . . . thus, I too" equals "my husband knows/has/can . . . thus, I too." Women who proudly declare themselves weak believe that weakness is an inherent part of goodness. And they believe that, just as they feel themselves too fragile to face the competitive professional workplace, the men who protect them feel too fragile to face the mysterious domestic world. For this reason, they believe they have the right to be materially cared for as long as they assume their full responsibility as guardians (or, as they prefer to think, caretakers) of the family's emotional life. They belong to the family but they are also co-owners of every family member, of his ideas, feelings, decisions and lives. They are goods that belong to the family but they also see themselves as owners of all family goods, people and things. In exchange for security and belonging, they give up intellectual capacity, social and professional advancement and economic independence to the men, loves and lords, who are in charge of them.

Michelle, the prestigious American attorney who suffers for her inexplicable love mismatches with Juan, the man she loves, was at the same gala event as Catherine. She couldn't resist commenting: "How could she? How can she stomach her husband's condescension? She graduated at the top of her class, she could have done anything, and now she accepts these comments without blinking an eye. If that's marriage, I'd rather be alone. I'd rather pay for my own luxuries than put up with that."

As a little girl, Michelle played alone on the beach. Year after year, during summer vacations, she played alone on the beach. She liked her mother and sisters and brothers to be close, but not so close that they interfered with her sandcastle building. Her family didn't understand that her greatest pleasure was giving people little gifts she had made, without asking anything in return but a smile.

Nothing more, but that grateful smile was everything to her. Michelle knew that everything she did she did in order to be more loved, in order to obtain that loving embrace that—she felt—never arrived in the moment or manner that fitted her precisely. She didn't care about the toys or candies that made her siblings happy. No material thing could assuage her profound need to be understood, could assuage her soul's hunger. She loved her family too much to let them know that she didn't like the smothering way they embraced her. She felt that she was the most sensible, the one who had to protect and worry about everyone because she was the best at decision-making. But she also felt that no one, not even her mother, knew what was best for her. She felt that she could not rely on anyone; that she could not herself love as if she didn't see that which no one else saw. If being loved required making oneself stupid, if feeling likeable and worthy of love meant being incompetent, then she would never be loved: she was not so weak as to be considered good by others.

Women like Michelle know themselves to be too strong, too determined to do as they like. For them it's certain that, usually, they know which are the best decisions, the best measures and means to take, both for themselves and for their romantic partners. They know how to love others better than others know how to love them. For others, these women are good, the best. And so it is very painful for these women to feel that in order to be loved by men they must cut off a piece of themselves, abandoning thereby their strength.

They don't want a relationship in which the other thinks for them; as when they were children, these women know that they think thoroughly and well. They seek partners who think as well as they do and who feel more competently. They want to learn from the emotional exchange of hearts that beat and feel in unison.

Unlike good weak women, women like Michelle know they're capable of surviving without the protection of a strong powerful man. Michelle and those like her are not afraid of facing the rough-and-tumble world of competitive power. But it is not worth to them to do whatever a man wants; they need men who can care for them properly by containing them in a precise embrace.

When they believe they've met such men, they feel so happy that they are scared of breaking the spell: they don't evaluate whether the offer comes from the arms of a man both strong and good or from one whose only pleasure is in being powerfully bad. Feeling themselves full of love produces such delight in them that they give themselves over to the feeling without consideration.

Let's imagine this encounter. A strong man is always intrigued by the romantic provocations of a woman who appears both strong and willing to let herself be trapped by him. Immediately, at the first signal, the inveterate hunter begins to set a trap for such a woman.

The first step of this dance consists of shared passion. Both feel successful: he, because he's embracing someone as he wants; she, because she feels embraced. The man—who doesn't doubt, who's convinced that he should lead—marks the rhythm of the next step in this sequence: they do what he wants. She accepts, delighted, seduced by the idea of being taken and sustained in the embrace of someone stronger than she. Until he begins to impose motions that she doesn't share, that don't correspond to the music to which she is dancing, that don't strike her as pertinent or adequate, that she doesn't consider good decisions. She refuses to accept what strikes her as arbitrary authority, open neither to discussion nor question. He insists: he won't consult her as to which steps to take, which spins to spin, which paths to follow. She doesn't tolerate his dominance and rebels: her movements show a brusque rhythmic change, a dramatic passage from passion to tension. Offended, she wonders, "Who does he think he is?" "Does he think I'm his slave?" "Doesn't he know who I am?" She begins to reject the choreographic commands that fascinated her before.

He becomes angry and stops dancing: "What are we about? Didn't you ask me to protect you, to hold you, to take you in hand? Didn't you tell me you wanted me to decide for you?" She gets scared and asks for forgiveness. She's afraid of being abandoned and of being, once again, without the longed-for embrace. She humiliates herself, she recants, she promises to obey him. They begin again to a rhythm of submission, a cadence that continues until she recovers her bodily memory: she remembers that she is not only good but also strong; her intelligence, independence, capacity for flight and leadership revive and so she wants to show him some steps of her own. He refuses to learn from her. "Who does she think I am?" "Does she know who's wearing the pants here?" He takes the last step, leaving the dance floor without explanation, leaving her with a disagreeable feeling of humiliation and asking herself why she's only interested in men whom she suspects from the start are incompatible with her, why she throws herself into affairs when she knows she's going to lose.

Why do dances between strong bad men and strong good women end badly? Because, unlike the men, these women move with both the efficiency of hunters and the tenacity of reapers. These women think of both future and present; they believe that love and passion can coexist. They want to feel, but they don't want to stop thinking.

The women don't want to mistrust or to protect themselves from those they love but neither do they want to transform themselves into hunted prey. The men, by contrast, find their attitude as bad men justified with these women: they believe that they are the only ones capable of halting the advance of these beings who think of themselves as independent, of showing the women that they're wrong, and of convincing them that they are in fact worse than the men. The men believe that the women are a bit more astute and quick than they are, a fact which makes the women the more dangerous. This 'masculine' strategy consists in finding behind hysteria and caprice 'feminine' susceptibility and sensibility that will let the men trap the women. The former are convinced that the latter, when they fall in love, fall like dominoes. But it's precisely at this moment that the men begin to strike the women as unbearable, this moment at which the women become fuelled with rancor and recrimination. The moral of these strong bad men is simple: one must never be trapped by a woman who doesn't know how to be 'femininely fragile', even as a little lie or romantic game.

Women like Michelle lose ground when they're with these men. It's true: these men don't love independent women; they only want those who like being their assistants, students or slaves. These women keep choosing these men because they think that, next time, they will know better how to protect themselves. But the next time, when it comes, women like Michelle can't tell whether they've picked professors, owners and lords *per se* or simply men who don't yet know how to be good without being weak. Full of self-doubt and recrimination, the women perpetuate the vicious circle in which they're trapped.

They're stubborn and they keep searching for strong good men. But they don't stop to learn from their mistakes. They don't realize that their emotional contradictions prevent them from recognizing the men they want or that these same contradictions prevent them from being recognized by such men. They don't suspect that some potential companions fled, feeling betrayed, abandoned, disillusioned and desperate: they thought they had found the strong good women they sought but then felt that in fact the women were bad.

Love is easier for women like Vanessa, who choose good weak men they can manipulate through fear and strength, and for women like Catherine, who choose strong bad men they can manipulate through guilt and goodness. These kinds of women resemble one another. Both resolve their emotional contradictions in the same way: they annul one of the two terms of the contradiction. They do not doubt, they do not fear, they do not feel guilty, they do not drown. Neither do they navigate or evolve: their ideas of feminine and masculine identity remain rigid and fixed.

For women like Andrea and Michelle—strong good women who are not prepared to infantilize or lobotomize themselves in order to reclaim their goodness, who are not prepared to transform themselves into fighters in order to recuperate their strength—love is much more difficult. These women's styles are different but their sentiments are similar: they doubt themselves and the other, they're scared of themselves and of the other, they feel guilty towards themselves and towards the other, they think they love too much or too little or that their men love too much or too little.

They navigate through and drown in unsatisfying relationships without ever reaching the security of answers to their pressing questions. How may women be 'femininely' strong? How may men be 'masculinely' good? How can a couple be both strong and good?

Sometimes they hold to a faith both overly cynical and overly ingenuous, a faith that allows them to maintain hope during their long difficult path. One of these women e-mailed the following prayer to her friends and colleagues:

> "*A oração de uma mulher*
> *Querido Senhor:*
> *Neste día de hoje, até o momento, eu estou fazendo tudo*
> *certinho.*
> *Eu não fofoquei, não perdi minha paciência,*
> *não fui avarenta, nem mal humorada, sórdida, insolente*
> *ou egoísta.*
> *Eu não lamentei, amaldiçoei ou comi chocolate.*
> *Porém, eu vou me levantar da cama em alguns minutos*
> *e eu precisarei muito de sua ajuda depois disso.*
> *Obrigada Senhor!*"

(A woman's prayer
Dear Lord:
Until now, I've done everything I was supposed to do.
I didn't lie or lose patience,

I was neither greedy nor ill-tempered nor small-minded
  nor insolent nor selfish.
I didn't pity myself, I didn't gossip or eat chocolate.
However, in a few minutes I'll get out of bed and
I'll need a lot of help immediately.
Thank you, Lord!)

This way of waiting for an encounter with a man—as if it were to do with a religious miracle—is very dangerous for strong women who still don't know how to be good.

8

THE INCONVENIENT EMBRACE

Maitena, a young Argentine humorist, has one of her characters say the following: "I dreamed of being a hard woman, of dedicating myself to something strange, of marrying an intense man and having a crazy life. It turns out that I'm crazy, I'm married to a strange man, I have an intense job and a hard life." I'm not the only mother who has more than once asked herself, faced with a daughter like Maitena, where she went wrong. Because that is how we feel when we see our intelligent, sensitive, complicated daughters suffer in relationships that strike us as utterly inadequate for them. We don't understand how, if our daughters were educated to be the best of their generation, they prefer losing loves with questionable men. How can we fail to worry when we see our daughters with intelligent bohemian poets who fail to make livings, or with married men who do not intend to divorce their wives, or with highly powerful impresarios who want our daughters to end their own professional lives in order to be perfect and servile collaborators?

Laura, an Argentine architect, met John, a young Chinese-American, in an urban anthropology course he was teaching and she, taking. At the end of the term, she returned to Argentina. During the time they spent in California and afterwards, while she was in Argentina and he in San Diego, she seemed to be very much in love. Numerous phone calls, long electronic letters, romantic trysts in out-of-the-way places marked this seemingly impossible love story. Until John began to prepare the paperwork for Laura's visa, which meant a marriage proposal and the possibility of a geographically stable relationship. Laura immediately backed off. In a phone call overheard by her disconcerted mother, she thanked John for his gesture but told him that she couldn't accept because she would never know if she had married him for love or for convenience. Laura and other women her age are so invested in finding a pure, true, romantic and impossible love that they make their own lives impossible in the arms of men who are not right for them.

Marina, an Italian economist, was very happy when Robert, a strong intriguing Australian businessman, stole her away from Marco, a good boring Italian she'd known since childhood. At first, Marina's parents rejected Robert: he struck them as dangerous, untrustworthy, overly interested in the conquest of women such as their daughter. Marina's friends felt abandoned by her, as she seemed delighted with the idea of moving to an unknown country to restart her life, without any professional connections and with the additional loss of a good position she'd obtained in her own city. During the months of difficulties with her family and friends, Marina seemed delighted, even euphoric: she was the chosen one. For love of her, Robert had decided to end his confirmed bachelorhood: he wanted to set up house, to have children with her. Marina's parents learned to love Robert, Marco forgave her: he decided that he'd rather marry Maria, another childhood friend with whom he had more in common. Happy ending? No. Marina began to overeat, to gain weight and to mistreat Robert, provoking him to leave her or stop loving her. She tried to explain why she was acting in this way, noting that neither her mother nor her friends understood. She wanted to stop being beautiful and intelligent, she wanted to stop accomplishing everything she set her mind on. To feel that others always did what she wanted scared her: she had conquered the strongest of men. If everyone did as she wanted, if a man as successful with women as Robert chose her, if her parents accepted her living abroad, if her childhood sweetheart remained her friend, if her girl friends promised to visit her, if the bank that employed her found a position for her in Sydney, Marina feared feeling supercilious. She feared becoming a monster, hated and envied by everyone. If she were ugly, if she knew how to provoke pity in her loved ones, if she felt more normal and more like her girl friends, her sisters, her mother . . .

To make a decision, whether in the economic or emotional realm, the professional or the private, one evaluates what will be won or lost with each possible option. The most sophisticated evaluations also incorporate data about how much will be won if one wins, how much will be lost if one loses.

Good men are not right for strong women who fear being bad; such women may transform themselves into bad women if the men turn out to be dully weak. Strong men are not right for these women either because such women may transform themselves into weak women if the men turn out to be dangerously bad. Since they are not happy in their love relationships neither with strong men nor with good ones, they end up convinced they can only aspire to receive the love of inconvenient men. For these women, the only Mr. Right is Mr. Wrong.

Mr. Wrong is Mr. Right—they believe—because both the strengths and weaknesses, the goodness and badness, can be predicted.

The inconveniences or problems vary: the man may be married, or a drug addict, or overly committed to his own ambitions, or overly wedded to his family's traditions and consequently neglectful of his beloved. Whatever the problems may be, they also fulfill the same function for women who, like Michelle, Laura, Andrea and Marina, doubt themselves: the problems give the women romantic certainties. Thanks to the patterned problems, the women continue to feel that they are strong and good rather than bad and weak.

While they maintain themselves in the confusion caused by their own multiplicities of being, they do not allow themselves to think through love; they merely return to the tools of credulity and distrust in order to make decisions about their romantic lives. Over and over, they choose unwisely, but, for these women, winning is losing. Only a hard strong woman, capable of being alone and of tolerating life's battles, can be good enough to tolerate the suffering caused by these relationships; only a strong woman can tolerate such suffering with the submissive resignation these women demonstrate.

With Mr. Wrong, these women can feel worried and serene, imprisoned and free, dependent and independent at once. To be misunderstood by their families and friends is a calculated and acceptable risk for them. In any case, they have never felt properly understood or conventionally accepted. By contrast, they have always felt themselves to be considered bizarre, eccentric or strange and so they have tried since they were little to accustom themselves to the idea that others' opinions do not matter to them. The problem here is that with Mr. Wrong, one sooner or later loses more than one gains. In some moment in the development of these relationships, the women will feel that they are weak and bad, insecure and anxious, vulnerable and imprisoned, beggars for or thieves of affection. And Mr. Wrong will cease to be Mr. Right.

This romantic choreography follows the same steps regardless of the particular problems of the dance partner. The dance begins when one of these women falls madly in love with a man who offers her an embrace that contains her entirely in the world of love but that does not contain her at all in the world of work. She revels in this embrace. In its intimacy, she feels good, soft, pliable with a feminine obedience because she does what he wants; she follows the steps that he imposes, from within his limitations. At the same time, she feels strong on the social scene: only an independent, determined, fierce woman can bear the limitations of this love with so much dignity.

For some time both partners are happy. Then the second step comes: she undergoes an epiphany regarding romantic surrender, one she had believed she would never experience, and agrees to pay any price for the privilege of feeling that she is a woman—a feeling given her for the first time in her life by this Mr. Wrong. She seems to need his embrace so much that he assumes she needs no demonstrations of his love other than those he chooses to give her. (Neither does she ask for any other such proofs.) He receives the best love at a rock-bottom price.

The third step in this dance occurs when she notices that the total embrace is delineated in time and space by the inconvenience or problem. She cannot manage to sustain the rhythm of altruistic, abnegated, good and at once passionate surrender that he asks of her. This relationship begins to strike her as insufficient, both in the world of power as in that of love. She wants more attention, more time, more care in the world of power than what he gives her: she feels tired, too burdened by the weight of a "masculine" life such as the one she lives. In the world of love she feels too needy and humiliated—too "feminine"—if she resigns herself passively to the crumbs of affection he tosses her.

In the fourth step, when she feels more weak he accuses her of being bad. She knew he was never going to leave his wife or get off drugs or find a stable job or separate himself from his family. She chose to love him in spite of the inconvenience that he never tried to hide. She notes that once again she is not womanly enough. She is not so docile as to obey him, believe in him, accept and satisfy without question the desires and needs of the man she loves.

The fifth step is definitive. She can declare herself bad and use her power to force him to renounce the problem, threatening him with abandonment if he refuses. Or she can declare herself weak, lopping off her strength and renouncing her own desires and needs in order to fit into the size of the embrace he is prepared to offer her, for fear of being left alone again.

I must confess that I know whereof I speak. In my own time, my relationship with Omar was such a love. In the first stage of our dance, thanks to his problem—a refusal to take any job in which he would feel subordinate—I was free to realize fully my professional life while he protected me, lovingly, within the home.

But later he told me that my involvement with the world of love struck him as insufficient; later, I began to feel alone and overly burdened with my responsibilities in the world of power.

Inconvenient loves alleviate the fear of being unloved that torment women who fear that they do not know how to love but— the repressed returns—these loves remind them at the same time that they've chosen so because they don't feel worthy of anything better.

These women, not knowing how to define themselves, feel that they are nothing. They believe that their ways of loving have always been abnormal, different from what one is supposed to feel. They do not have the consolation of simultaneous or successive relationships with various men, such as some of us turned to in our own confusion. They want to be completely loved by one man, in one time and place, both supposed to be endless.

Nevertheless, the receipt of the desired emotional demonstration provokes sorrow rather than joy. They recoil if the men they love seem ready to offer them love. "What?" They think. "Doesn't he know that I'm strange and difficult, that no one and nothing can ever contain me entirely?" They suppose that the men must be relating to an illusion: "He definitely doesn't know who I am yet," they argue, or, "He must be hiding some problem from me." These sentences express the women's conviction that the unique, complete and total love they desire does not exist and never will.

They feel strange because they do not enjoy manipulative strategies in their romantic lives. They are not interested in an encounter in which the winner is he who doesn't show his hand, who gives less love, who best hides his feelings, who most doubts the other. For these women, competition—who distrusts first, who discovers the other's plans most quickly, who manipulates more and better—does not function as an erotic stimulus. They neither know how nor care to use mystery or intrigue as mean of seduction. They do not enjoy relationships that require them to distrust their partner or in which they themselves are objects of suspicion. They prefer the crude, brutal and truthful transparency of desire to the slow agonizing dance of mistrust and credulity.

They fear receiving a romantic offer that exceeds their expectations, because they always pay excessively for what they get. Their desperate desire to be good without losing their strength obliges them to try to be, always, the best of the best. If they get what they ask for—and they ask for a lot—they fear feeling suffocated by their own ethical commitments, and of giving back too much. For this reason, it is convenient for them when some external limit makes the romantic offer an inconvenient one.

They feel guilty for being strong—read unintentionally bad— if an available man, whom they like, shows his interest in them. So they react with timidity, shame or rejection towards any emotional demonstration made them before an audience. They prefer that such a man not pick them. They fear so not to love him enough as much as they fear that he will love them too much. They don't know how to assure themselves that he is truly good, and not a weakling that will end up being a bad person for them. How can they know that he is not lying, not wearing a mask of honesty? How can they be sure? After much anguish, they decide that it is better for them to surrender themselves to a man unquestionably and visibly unavailable.

He poses no danger, they think. There is no risk of confusion. Unavailable loves work because they take advantage of hypocrisy. The women, wanting to believe in love but fearing their own excessive credulity, suppose that a man who asks to be loved despite his unavailability cannot disillusion them. When he confesses that he cannot give them everything, they hear that he will give all he can; when he does not hide his own dishonesty, they consider him to be honest.

For women who doubt themselves—they believe— unavailable men are good prospects because the women do not risk being bad. They don't fear their own betrayal or abandonment of him, they don't run the risk of being the one who loves less or trusts less: it is already clear that the man loves less and that this lack is due to external causes. Unavailable loves guarantee that these women are good. In this type of romantic choreography, the strong woman ends up being the one who loves more, who is more generous, who is more prepared to do what the other wants. The apparent disadvantage becomes an advantage because, in the world of love, giving is better than receiving: he who loves more, surrenders more and gives more controls the embrace.

To love completely the man who never surrenders completely allows these women to feel tenderness in their souls, softness in their bodies, calm in their minds—and to remain free. For no matter how much these women renounce, given their love of someone unavailable, this love at the same time lets them refute a belief they have held about themselves since childhood: that they do not know hot to feel as they should. Finally they love as they suppose women love: resignedly, passively, obediently, submissively. They feel embraceable because they discover that they know how, that they can embrace: the unavailable man liberates them from themselves.

With him they don't feel weak, because he convinces them that they and they alone understand him so well, embrace him with such passion, and see him so clearly. They feel worthy of being loved, as only they can offer the strong love he needs. They become enthusiastic about this love because they are unique. The unavailable man recognizes this uniqueness and rewards it, placing them in a unique location: for being so good, they are the most loved; for being so strong, they are the least cared for.

He must be a strong man in order to attract a strong woman, one who will be excited by having to overcome difficulties. The unavailable love requires all her skills as a good huntress, without the risk of killing the prey. To the benefit of both, this man lets himself be caught out in his games and weaknesses. It is for them a delicious dance in which the strong woman can be strong because she knows that the partner's problem will dominate her strength, rendering it less dangerous, and in which the strong man embraces and lets himself be embraced by an equal, knowing that his unavailability makes him invulnerable to her.

This class of men is the only one that understands strong women who wish to be good, according to such women. The men sense the women from a distance, they recognize them as equals. The women reward the men thinking that they are the only companions, comrades, partners who can keep up. The men surprise them, catch them up, invade them, soften them. The men do not fear them: they do as they wish with them. The men take the reins from the women who have been wanting to give them up. Unavailable men are good prospects for these women when the latter want to feel docile, domesticated, obedient: when they want to feel that they are women like all the other women.

They convince themselves that they cannot hurt him even if they use maximally all their powers and forces; they cannot hurt him, they think, even with the most indomitable aspects of their personalities. For nothing is more indomitable than the inconvenience with which he is burdened and which acts, for both, as a defensive shield. Some women prefer this kind of relationship because it removes all the danger of the act of giving free rein to their emotions. Such women know that even if they gallop like wild horses, even if they go mad from passion (which they have never yet done, for fear of being unstoppable), the external problem will act as a brake, limiting the flourishing of their force. Within these rigid limits, they can be limitlessly free.

Unavailable men always make clear that they do not need these women. They insist that they are with them only because they want to be, because they love them. And so the women think that this kind of love is the only true, freely given kind. The trust is absolute: romantic mistrust cannot enter this walled city, think the women. Within this walled city, this time outside time, the women manage the longed-for surrender. They know that this love is limited, circumscribed, but this limit is also the guarantee of the liberty which lets them inhabit without doubt the romantic terrain.

They are prepared to pay any price to escape the curse with which they feel they have been burdened: "She's so smart that no man can stand her," "She's so self-sufficient that she doesn't need anyone," they have heard since they were little. Unavailable men seem smarter or stronger than they. The women cannot solve the insuperable problems that prevent them from doing just as they please with the men, and so these problems remind them that their will cannot accomplish everything. They feel, then, human, equal to other women. They learn that they cannot always attain whatever they want, as they grew up believing. They learn that there exists someone who might know how to contain them, dominate them, house them; someone who might know how to make them feel the desire to embrace and to be embraced. Someone who moves them, who takes them out of the fortress they constructed in order to defend themselves from the fear of feeling loved without knowing how to love in return.

With an unavailable man, illusions don't exist: there is thus no reason to distrust him. From the start, the women know that this choreography will end badly and will confirm that love is impossible. A relationship that begins without hope can never disappoint. The women already know that they cannot aspire to a happy love because of their own strangeness. Inconvenient loves let them, at least, feel that they fail not because they don't know how to love, or because they love less than they should. On the contrary, they convince themselves: they lose because they love too much, without caution, without calculation.

The unavailable man helps these women realize a cherished dream: he lets strong women think and feel, live in intimacy and in the world, feel themselves both free and in relation to another, be tender as women and strong as men at once. He disarms them: he removes the dangerous force of their intelligence, letting them bask in the goodness which is also theirs. They win by being unable to win, by being unable to overcome the obstacle to the man's availability: no one could accuse them of being bad. Although it is not the role they would choose, the weak and tender victim role, firmly embraced by their strong victimizer, is the one played by women in these relationships.

Whatever the form taken by the man's unavailability, this kind of love works for women who cannot stop being strong but who cannot stand bad men. Thanks to the strong, good man who suffers an inconvenience, these women can be strong and good at once. But the costs of such loves are sky-high: so high that, after a time, such loves no longer work. It is usually the case that women who choose these kinds of choreographies end up hating themselves for having so chosen.

Liz, an American lawyer who always thought she didn't know how to love because she's exercised the skill of discovering others' defects since childhood, surprises her family and her friends when she declares she's madly in love with Larry, an aggressive businessman, as well American, well known for his romantic cynicism. He affirms that love does not exist and defies anyone to prove him of the contrary. Liz is delighted with the chance of being herself—precisely she who does not know if she knows how to love—the one to convince him that this surrender in love is worth something. She accepts the challenge. She may use all her strength to show him that he is mistaken, giving him so much love that—so she thinks—he will have no other choice but to heal his cynicism. Liz does not doubt: she who never abandons her alert positioning nor her hunting skills to detect danger, falls in the trap of an inconvenient man and believes that, finally, she found love—or better still, that love found her. That is why neither her family nor her friends understand why she's in panic when he confesses that he loves her, that he feels cured of his loving skepticism and starts making plans for a happy future together. Nobody understands why Liz feels out of control, unstoppable and un-embraceable if the inconvenience disappears and he falls in love with her—that is, if he stops being the one who defends in a stronger way within the couple. Liz doesn't tell anyone she's afraid that if she succeeds in Larry abandoning his cynicism, she will be able to convince him of anything, and so she will feel prisioner of her own cynicism—that which makes her think everyone else is weaker (more in need of love) than her.

Liz prefers that Larry loved her but that he wouldn't marry her. She'd rather he'd maintain, true to his declared love skepticism, the lack of conviction in the advantages of marriage. In this way, she could keep with him a love relationship without confinement, with personal space and freedom. She could believe in love without fear of being imprisoned in love. She would rather feel that he chooses her simply because, because of her strangeness, her lack of familiarity and convention, her refusal to demand from him any responsibility other than the love that she, and only she, inspires him, and not because she's a good candidate to marriage, a convenient woman.

After many years of unsatisfactory love relationships, Margarita, an Argentinean psychologist living in New York, feels she found the love of her life. The only inconvenience is that Joaquín, a delightful Spanish sociologist, her colleague in post-graduate studies, says he is a well-married man. He shows her he is stronger than her because he desires to be with her, but doesn't need to be with her. For him the furtive and scattered love encounters he maintains with Margarita are a luxury, an intellectual exquisiteness his wife cannot offer him. It is a love so special that only deserves to be enjoyed in special occasions. Margarita suffers: for her the encounters with Joaquín have become a daily necessity. Nevertheless, she insists in keeping this unsatisfactory love relationship: it is hard for her to confess that it is convenient for her that he cannot see her with the frequency that she says she needs, because Joaquín's temporal limitations allow her to dedicate herself to her studies, her friends, her professional ambitions. If he wanted to marry her, Margarita wouldn't have that time and all her life would revolve around him, as his wife's does now. In the end, the fact that he needs her less confronts her with her feminine need to be embraced, with the emotional hole, with the emotional dependency that the relationship both calms and augments. Wanting him, waiting for him, longing for his presence lets her feel that she is good when she discovers herself loving. But wanting him, waiting for him, longing for his presence also make her feel that she is weak, needing a love that she does not receive.

Sebastián is a Nicaraguan poet who just arrived to New York, a young man who strongly maintains his attitude of activist of rebellion against all social formalities. He prefers to be a waiter in a fashionable restaurant, where he gets substantial tips, rather than earn less working as a phantom writer for a compatriot friend of his father who's been living in the United States for a long time. Sebastián defends with such conviction his love for poetry and bears all rejection to his work with such integrity and dignity that María, a successful Puerto Rican graphic designer educated in New York, admires him, envies him and falls in love with him. Next to him, she feels contained, understood and accompanied for the first time in her life. He reveals to her the hypocrisy of the world of power in which she must disguise herself to maintain her status, and he teaches her how to enjoy the liberty of the world of love, a liberty neither bought nor sold. Sometimes, this love brings her to an abundant happiness. But sometimes this love leads her to the most profound desperation. Because of him she feels inadequate in her friendships, in her family, and in her professional relationships. When he refuses to stop being himself and demands that she accepts him as he is, that she accepts his refusal to enter the world of power, she will confront her own fears, ambivalences, and social shames. And then the love that has so strengthened her will begin to weaken her.

If the women who choose inconvenient loves don't overcome the obstacle present in these relationships, they feel weak and humiliated, condemned to join the ranks of women mistreated by men and like those ranks to be dependent, resentful, melancholic and empty. But if they do overcome the obstacle, they feel bad, authoritarian, bossy, condemned to join the ranks of those women who use poor good men to satisfy their masculine desires to hunt and like those ranks to be invasive, hard, insensitive, selfish, and overly masculine.

Ultimately, inconvenient loves are not so convenient. The unavailable man gives the woman time and space to live her own life, but he also abandons her. He does not impose on her a boring routine life but neither does he offer her any security. He is not scared by her tantrums, silences or impetuous decisions, but neither does he restrain such actions in himself. He offers her the freedom to be as she is, with her impassioned intelligence, her irreverence and her sense of humor. He offers an embrace that defies categorization, as he—like she—is neither good nor bad, strong nor weak, and so is able to liberate her from her eternal uncomfortable sensation of strangeness. But at the same time he condemns her to the strangeness of this love that resists categorization; that does not occur in the same time and space as normal daily life, because, unlike her, he does not care to overcome the confusion of his feelings.

When these inconvenient loves fail, strong good women are left feeling bad and weak and, because of that, they believe that they will never find the precise embrace they seek. They don't know how to look for this longed-for embrace, an embrace that knows the exact measure of what they hope for, that does not promise them all the answers but permits them all the questions, that liberates them fully and finally from the feeling of strangeness that has been with them always.

But some rebel against this defeat. They have failed, yes, but they are still alive. With the same emotional contradiction with which they began their search, they encourage themselves to continue. If they are so strange, they should not seek an equally strange embrace. They should not seek an indefinable embrace, like that offered by an unavailable love, nor a bifurcated embrace, like that offered by a partial love, nor an ephemeral embrace, like that offered by a love first credulous and then distrustful. They should seek—and in the case of these rebels do seek—a complete, paradoxical, multifaceted, unique embrace, one offered by a love capable of being strong and good at the same time and with the same intensity.

9

Syncretic Loves

Paula was six years old when the nightmare that would haunt her for years to come appeared for the first time.

We lived in Rio then—Paula, her older sister Natasha, and I—but at that time only Paula spoke Portuguese fluently. In her dream, she saw a devil and an angel fighting over her. The devil told her to harm her sister and me because we spoke a different language (Spanish, instead of her near-native Portuguese) and because we made her feel alien. For the devil, speaking Spanish also meant speaking the language of the conformist, the submissive; the establishment. The angel, by contrast, told her to protect and care for us because we didn't understand Portuguese and because we were not like her. For the angel, speaking Portuguese also meant speaking the language of the nonconformist, the rebel; the marginal.

Paula's devil and angel appear in her dreams and in her emotional conflicts whenever she feels misunderstood, under-nurtured, or poorly loved. She hears one version of her voice telling her to be good by protecting and forgiving those whom she thinks are weaker than she (as both her sister and I were during Paula's childhood); at the same time, and with the same intensity, she hears another version of her voice telling her to be strong by defending herself against those whom she thinks are worse than she and who want to harm her. Paula herself lives

147

neither in the conformity of the establishment nor in the rebellion of the margins, neither in the angel's world nor in the devil's.

Paula is not alone in this violent painful debate with herself. Many women her age feel the presence in themselves of 'two distinct beings, two opposing principles, as the Bible say, struggling with each other,' as Marcos, my mother's spurned suitor, phrased it. "They are not cleanly separated from one another but instead may become confused and mixed, giving rise to a hybrid neither good nor bad. This new being, composed of two parts, can scarcely be said to exist, and because it possesses characteristics of each without being wholly one or the other, it may be hard to understand." Like Marcos, many women my daughters' age know that 'it is precisely this spiritual indecision that provokes the most suffering.' Emotionally bilingual, they do not know where, when, to whom or why to speak one language or the other.

The suffering grows because they don't know when they should protect the other and when themselves; when they are loved for being strong and when hated for being bad; when they are loved for being good and when scorned for being weak; when they are good as opposed to only weak, when they are bad as opposed to only strong. They repeat without question the emotional lessons learned in childhood: they act as if they think that the strong are bad and the good, weak, although they don't actually believe this. And, because they obey contradictory teachings that question one another, the women make mistakes: they attack or they protect, they let themselves be attacked or protected by the wrong people, in inopportune moments, for erroneous reasons.

Some women of my daughters' generation do not manage to come out of the vicious circles created by the emotional contradictions they learned with their mothers and the societies they grew up in: either they get sick with *Amorous Mistrusts and Credulities* and they drown in *Inconvenient Embraces* or they resort to drastic emotional surgeries in order to avoid the repeated romantic miss-encounters and they abandon some of the *Split Loves*. They split themselves in halves: some choose the teachings of the love of power, exaggerating their bad sides in order to stay strong and avoid the dangers of the asphyxiating dependence to love. Others choose to follow the teachings of the power of love: they exaggerate their weaknesses in order to stay good and avoid the dangers of the independent but solitary love.

Other, more ambitious, women, are not ready to conform to dichotomous, partial, split, emotional destinies. They seek to relate to a good and strong man who understands them completely and holds them in a *Precise Embrace*.

They do not understand why they have not found it yet. They cannot understand why they lose in the world of love if they feel they are the best in all other aspects of life. It is not enough for them to seek an escape goat, to accuse men or themselves of 'lack of love' or 'fear of emotional attachments.' It is not enough for them to think that men prefer weak women whom they can manipulate—not realizing that it is the other way around—or that let themselves be manipulated by bad women. And, even if these were the only possible love strategies, these women are not ready to use them to hunt for men. They do not want to believe that all men may be so stupid. They prefer to keep on searching for that man who seems different. They resist emotional conformism: "It is best to be alone than in bad company," is the lemma they have learned with their strong mothers. It is also not useful for them to think they ask too much: they were educated to want the best of everything, the best in everything, always. They persist in their ideas about love: they are convinced that the love they wish is the best love. Nothing will make them give up their search.

They want to know how and why love miss-encounters happen. They are ready to know the truth, even if it is a painful one for them.

They want to understand why sometimes they act like emotional beggars and others like thieves with people whose love they long for; why, even if they think they love this people, sometimes they feel they hate them because they are bad and others because they are weak; why sometimes they think they do not need anything from anyone and other times think that they cannot live without the other's embrace; why sometimes they feel that they are utterly depraved and other times that they are utterly stupid, when they know that they are neither one nor the other. They want to understand why, even though inside they feel emotionally strong and good, outside they act as if they were the exact opposite: sometimes as the bad ones, others as the weak ones. They want to understand.

They are interested in having with men an emotional accountability that is neat and that follows a more trustworthy criteria than emotional despair. They imagine that this will allow them to see what they are doing for men not to understand them and, if they manage to express their feelings with greater precision, they will correct further emotional misunderstandings. If they win, according to this love ideology, they win a lot: to be loved by a strong and good man who they so longed to find. But, even if they lose, they still win: they stop condemning themselves for believing they are bad or weak, thinking that they are sick or emotional failures, feeling incapable of loving 'as they should' and difficult to be loved as they wished. Maybe they will continue not to be understood by the men they love and by whom they are loved, but for sure they will love and understand themselves more.

These women are neither good nor bad nor strong nor weak but entirely the contrary, and, while they do not love as one is supposed to, neither can they explain how they do love. They act as if they are bad or weak knowing that they are neither: they prefer so instead of being considered strange, unassimilable, sick, too emotionally complicated. They want to be somebody, to claim some identity, even if that identity is condemned. And such has been the case since their girlhoods.

Alessandra says: "I cried every time my parents went out. They thought I was scared to be left alone, but actually I was terrified that something would happen to them. I saw them as so fragile . . . And I suffered because the idea that everything ends prevented me from enjoying anything. I was always scared of death and these themes never left me but I didn't speak with anyone about them. They didn't understand me and they treated me as if I were insatiably needy, a bottomless pit. They gave me all they could but they couldn't give me what I needed, because I couldn't explain my feelings."

Paula, Alessandra and other women like them feel sometimes diabolical and sometimes angelic because they were born with a binocular emotional gaze: they look at life; they think and feel, at the same time and with the same intensity, as strong and good: they never surrender and they always trust.

They do not surrender because they know that everyone, including they themselves, is limited or flawed in some ways. They perceive the impenetrability of every body, the opacity of every soul, the finite quality of time and the narrow confines of human space. They know the meaning of the words precarious, ephemeral, contingent, and relative, and they know that these words bind the world of the emotions as much as the world of ideas. They neither can nor wish to stop thinking. They neither can nor wish to surrender ingenuously to the illusory power of love, nor follow the law of eternal salvation by dissolving in the other's embrace.

They always trust because, at the same time and with the same intensity they know that every human being—including they themselves—contains within himself potential perfection. They know the meaning of the words eternal, definite, essential, and unconditional, and they know that these words bind the world of the emotions as much as that of ideas. Their intuition lets them perceive the open pathways of each body, the porosity of every soul, the immensity of time and the amplitude of human space. For them, emotional empathy is as strong as existential solitude. They neither can nor wish to stop feeling. They neither can nor wish to surrender cynically to the love of power, nor to follow the law of the jungle, dissolving the other in their arms. They need the other's embrace in order to be able to tolerate the pain of daily little deaths.

They do not idealize but they do trust, they know of death but believe in life, they recognize human imperfections and sustain a desire for excellence. They think what they feel and feel what they think; they have done so since they were little. They have known since they were little that everything is relative: thinking relativists their feelings and feeling relativists their thoughts. They neither love nor hate with impassioned fanaticism because they know that every thought, every feeling, every truth is relative: each is formed in relationship and depends for its existence on various gazes from various places. Since they were little, these women have loved their mothers, but they recognize their defects; they have recognized those of their fathers and loved them. They please themselves when they are strong and capable of using their own resources to go through life; they displease themselves when they feel that they are capable of being bad, of doing as they wish, of alleviating dangers they've provoked. They please themselves when they are good and know how to care for others, when they do as the other wishes; but they displease themselves when they feel weak, incapable of managing to find the embrace they want, impotent in resolving romantic conflicts.

They know that they want a lot but do not believe that they want too much. Their desire for a love both powerful and affectionate, free and secure, sensual and tender, sensitive and intelligent, mysterious and predictable, does not strike them as excessive. They know that, for them, the choice is not between believing or not believing in love, between ingenuity or distrust, between security and liberty, between symbiosis and individuality.

They know that their emotional needs cannot be met with objects, even if these are the most extravagant and expensive gifts, nor with extravagant praise (they know their own defects too well), nor with stifling signs of admiration (they want to stop being the ones who are always more than capable.)

Some women my daughters' age know that they are neither 'masculinely' strong nor 'femininely' good: they know that they are strange and indefinable in their ways of loving, thinking and feeling. They know, in short, that they are emotionally bilingual.

But they don't know that it is impossible to understand them when they express, in a dizzying and disordered and encoded manner, all their thoughts and feelings at once. They don't know that, for those who listen to them, even for those interlocutors who love them and who wish to understand them; their entangled ways of loving and of asking for love are unintelligible.

They have suffered since they were little because they often receive the opposite of what they ask for: often they are rejected by those by whom they wish to be loved and chosen by those whom they reject. They often end up so misunderstood by others that, without understanding how or why, they end up allied to their enemies and ranged against their friends.

They ask, simply, for understanding, but the response they often get is a gaze of pity or fear.

They don't know why they can't find the desired complicity, why the ardently longed-for intimacy is so elusive for them. Neither they nor those who love them know that the embrace they seek is that which responds with an attention and empathy able to understand what each and every one of their little angels and devils wants, needs or claims. These women don't know that sometimes they don't receive the embrace that would bring them emotional satisfaction because they don't know what it is they needed or how to ask for it.

The more irritated they get when others don't understand them, the worse they feel and the less able they are to make themselves understood: they enclose themselves more within themselves. The more they need the other's understanding, the more difficult it is for them to explain their longings to be understood as they are and so their fear that these longings will remain always unseated grows.

These women lead a double life, emotionally speaking. They do not lie—the love of truth was born with them and within them—but, in order to avoid scaring or harming their loved ones, or being harmed by them, they hide what they feel: they think that they must be dangerous and terribly strange if not even those who love them can understand them. Laurie, a young psychologist born and raised in Los Angeles within a family that tried to keep unchanged the Indian traditions from their ancestors, explains: "I grew up feeling like a stranger and living as if I were part of a minority within my own community. I wasn't exactly a stranger, but I wasn't like the rest of my family or my friends' families. I was interested in other things than my mother, my father, my sister and 98% of my classmates. I was too respectful to marginalize myself entirely but too different to adapt entirely."

Laurie ended up developing a private world, which she defines as 'a secret life in limbo.' "I have watched myself living since I was a girl. I've never fit in; I've always been both present in and absent from the places in which my life takes place. To feel less alone, I developed an interior voice that kept me company; I know it's my own voice but I experience it as if it were the voice of someone who understands me better than I myself do: the voice calms me, consoles me, corrects me. I can't be guided by the advice of others who don't know who I am. My sister thinks I'm a lesbian and my mother thinks I'm perfect while treating me sometimes as if I were a monster. They don't know who I am."

To protect her family and herself, she never told them about her goings about in the world, when she began to look for romantic partners. "Because, despite feeling unique and unable to mix with the majority, I always thought that there must be others like myself. But I felt very alone, very scared of getting lost. It was quite strange: on the one hand, I felt bad about living this secret life; on the other hand, I became enraged at my mother who in a way forced me to live in this way. She neither understood me nor accepted that I was different from her and my sister and my cousins."

This secret and private space of limbo protects women such as Laurie from the critical gazes of those who love them, but such a space also locks them into the role of familiar black sheep. Aggression (from people who loves but fears them, because of their differences) doesn't reach these women in limbo, but neither do the embraces of those who, loving them, are prepared to try to understand.

In limbo, alone, they let their affects soar and they liberate their feelings: they create their own cocoon, a powerful loving womb that soothes their particular wounds, calms their painful doubts; binds their lacerating contradictions. Like birds, these women know how to protect their nest with bits of embraces they've received from their mothers, their grandmothers, an aunt, a friend of their mother's. Some of us had contradictory affects because our emotional migration led us to live with hearts divided between the world of work and the world of home—but we always knew that we had not yet reached a port. And, amidst the turbulent emotional contradictions and maddening double messages we've bequeathed our daughters, we've also bequeathed them, in an almost inaudible voice, our desires that they continue to seek their own authentic selves.

In limbo, our daughters can forget our contradictory words and re-encounter our sincere, clean, whole, precise embraces. In limbo, our daughters can hear inside themselves a syncretic emotion, one difficult to decipher if one doesn't know how to crack the code. I borrow a phrase from the Spanish poet Gabriel Celaya, in order to name as 'a pulse beating in the dark' the frustrating feeling caused by those who 'scarcely let us say that we are who we are,' suffered by some of our daughters. They feel this way and understand a lot about their mothers: good women who didn't want to be weak, women who acted as if they were bad in order to feel strong.

In limbo, emotions do not stupefy our daughters: they intuit that we seemed dishonest because we did not know how to escape our contradictions. And they also intuit that we were sincere in our attempts to respect them more than adults normally respect children. They know that we gave them the freedom to decide for themselves, the right to defend their own opinions, space to investigate their own desires. In limbo, they take refuge in this love that was at times too rational, at times too cold and distant, but that was truthful and exact in its respectful intentions. They remember the precise embrace that existed once, in a fleeting tiny scene that was, nevertheless, real for them.

Nevertheless, out of limbo, when they try to relate to others, these women find that their partners don't understand that they are strong while wanting to be good. And neither have we, their mothers, understood them. But they don't see that we cannot understand them because they do not tolerate feeling so different from us, from their peers, from their partners; they do not tolerate feeling so alone in their ways of thinking and feeling. They prefer to think that they are wrong, that they are strange, sick or crazy. Or to hide their true feelings, to masquerade. Or to doubt themselves: surely they do not love as one ought. How else to explain, other than by recourse to insanity or illness, the faults of which they are accused by those who do not understand them or the mistakes they do make, without wanting to, without being able to avoid them, when they don't feel understood as they need to be understood?

They doubt themselves because they don't realize that their emotional difficulties are caused by the dizzying, illogical and confused way in which their emotions appear to those who cannot read or understand their paradoxical feelings. They don't realize that they have become emotionally syncretic.

According to the dictionary, syncretism "is a philosophical system that tries to reconcile different doctrines." Other definitions include: "the combination of different forms of belief or practice; the result of the attempt to harmonize elements of various origins without having logical unity as a goal." Generally, the term is used to refer to cultural or religious syncretism; here, it refers to a combination of elements of the emotions. But emotional syncretes go the dictionary one better: in their ardent desire for both harmony and unity, they strive towards a syncretism that is both precise and highly coherent.

They place themselves in the front line, exposing themselves to the dangers that are hidden in the path towards the search for their own emotional truths. They tolerate loneliness and they dare not be like their mothers, their generational peers or their eventual partners. They embark on the work of elucidating, arranging, organizing and making explicit the emotional syncretisms that define them, separating themselves definitively from the split emotions that they've combined. They bear the pain of being accused of betraying both those who gave birth to them and their peers.

Laurie says: "When I began to talk, I felt the words running around crazily in my head as if they were a bunch of wild horses. They ran faster than my thoughts and than my voice; they clogged my throat, I couldn't breathe, my mother scolded me because she was scared that I would choke, I got very nervous and the words I wanted to use to make myself understood ran around even more quickly in my head. And my mother got even angrier because of her fear of my choking. I became desperate because she didn't understand me and I ended up shouting and muttering, inarticulately."

Many women of my generation and many men of my daughters' generation are frightened by these women's way of loving. We flee their implacable gazes; we don't understand their ways of embracing or wanting to be embraced. We feel too much in demand that too much is required of us that we are made too responsible for not giving them the love they require. But we don't always accept the task of being impeccable mirrors for them. To defend ourselves against the charge of not loving them enough, we accuse them of being too avid or too pretentious. It's always easier to blame the other. So when the mothers or partners of these women feel unjustly criticized, and when we feel that, despite our efforts, they do not concede anything, we return their criticism: they're at fault for our inability to embrace them.

We do not recognize them: worse, we negate them. We, their mothers, renounce some of our daughters, despite our having planted in them the desire for progress and the desire to remain free of any kind of tie. And the men who most interest them renounce them, despite having encouraged them to be as they are by claiming that they are more attracted to women who don't seem easy to entrap.

We encourage them to be good but, when they are, we accuse them of being weak. When we, their mothers or the men who are their potential partners cannot love them, we say it is their fault. This thought calms our consciences but it does not resolve the problem. We go along without understanding the whirlwind of thoughts and feelings that inhabits their minds and hearts.

And, as the problem is never resolved and we continue not to understand them, these women, in order to be embraced, have no other option but to fit themselves into the available embraces: those which are offered to pitiful weak people or to repentant bad people.

Outside limbo, they can receive our heartfelt embrace when their strength has been used up and their defensive capacities have been run through. Some mothers and some men only know how to embrace these women when they feel so anguished by their defeats that we suffer along with them. They can also count on our rigorous embrace when they so fear losing control of their own aggressions that we stop respecting them, we stop fearing them and we manage to approach them.

When their romantic searches fail and they don't understand why, when they can't stand themselves any longer and feel that they are too weak or too bad, too restrained or too out of control, these women content themselves with crumbs of affection or with reprimands disguised as love. They act as if they are either beggars or sinners. They do not yet know that they are emotional syncretes who have not taken the time to untangle patiently their confused emotions, nor to understand how or why they've joined contradictory feelings.

These women are not culpable of our—their mothers' or their partners'—inability to love them as they need to be loved. But they are responsible for differentiating between those times when we do not give them the love they need because we do not wish to and those times when we don't know how to: they will not encounter the precise embrace as long as they don't know how to ask for it; as long as they cannot explain how they love and how they need to be loved; as long as they don't know how to distinguish between romantic miss-encounters that are due to misunderstandings and those that are due to lack of love; as long as they do not discriminate between those requests dictated by intelligent devils and those dictated by insipid angels and those dictated by their complex and as-yet too dizzying emotional needs.

Some take longer than others to unravel and understand their affects. Some take longer than others to realize that when they let anger invade them because their mothers and partners do not understand them, they are not strong but rather too weak: they only react to our actions. They lag in understanding that when they are invaded by guilt for having attacked us in order to defend themselves from our attacks, they are not bad but rather too good: they accept all the responsibility for the miss-encounter.

It is hard for them to accept that they act as if they are both, strong and weak, bad and good, because they are following the steps of the contradictory romantic choreographies of those who love them and by whom they wish to be loved.

Each generation encourages the next generation to progress beyond itself. Progress brings change: abandonment, betrayal, the rejection of older lifestyles. Expectations, desires and needs change from generation to generation, as do definitions of happiness. Ways of thinking, feeling and acting change even within a family. From mothers to daughters, fathers to sons, identities and ways of being change. Generational distances and misunderstandings are inevitable, but some of these hurt more than others. When some women of my mother's generation transformed themselves into *gauchas-judías* in Argentina (or Italian-Americans in the United States or Afro-Brazilians in Brazil), inaugurating a cultural syncretism, they knew they could not count on their mothers to learn the new languages or cultural customs. But they never doubted their mothers' embraces. They might reject them, scorn them or abandon them, but they were there, clear, definite, unconditional and always available for the daughters.

When some women of my generation transformed themselves into professional women, inaugurating a workplace syncretism, we knew that we could not count on our mothers in order to feel understood in our professional soaring. But we never doubted our mothers' embraces. We might reject them, scorn them or abandon them, but they were there, clear, definite, unconditional and always available for us. Our mothers did not understand us, but they admired our ways of being women.

But the difficulties in comprehension between women my daughters' age, who have inaugurated an emotional syncretism, and their mothers are more brutal, painful and difficult to tolerate than what we suffered with our own mothers.

In the work world, we and our daughters are equally strong and good. Although we don't work solely for economic compensation, both they and we are professional women and as such we understand each other, respect each other, embrace each other and learn from one another. We feel mutually proud, loved and lovable in our intellectual roles. We inhabit the same professional space.

But we inhabit different emotional worlds. Some of our daughters want a total love—one which we ourselves taught them to want—but we only know how to practice a piecemeal love that condemns them to a life of wandering. We don't understand them; they become enraged at us because we don't understand them, we become enraged at them because we don't understand them. And so neither mothers nor daughters feel loved as we wish to be loved.

Some women my daughters' age fear being condemned never to love or to be loved as they wish: if not even their own mothers understand them as they are, perhaps their embrace will never reach another nor will they ever be embraced as they need to be.

They still don't know that their affects are dizzying because it is as impossible to obey as to disobey a contradiction: if one disobeys one element of a contradictory equation, one obeys the other, inexorably.

The fact is that, as they obey us or try to disobey us, daughters of contradictory mothers like me cannot help but repeat with their romantic partners the contradictory, ambivalent and erratic relationships that they have maintained and continue to maintain with us. They cannot imitate us in everything nor oppose themselves to us completely. They cannot do what those women who do not have and have never had ambivalent relationships with their mothers do: repeat or change completely some romantic ideology. They will never be the proud legatees of those women who knew how to be excellent warriors in the world of power nor of those women who knew how to be excellent geishas in the world of love nor of those who vindicated the memory of their embattled or humiliated mothers. We, their contradictory mothers, were sometimes excellent fighters and sometimes excellent geishas. But we were never proud of our contradictory ways of loving; we were particularly troubled by our contradictory forms of maternal love. And so we never taught them that they could be proud of their own strange, paradoxical, multifaceted way of loving.

Neither were we so defeated or humiliated in the romantic terrain that our daughters could mount the barricades for us without knowing that they were exaggerating. They know, even though we often tried to make them believe otherwise, that we did not always put up with being victimized by bad men. They know that sometimes we were the victors. And, in honor of truth, women who seek emotional justice seek an impeccable love, in which neither victors nor victims exist. But we, their mothers, did not know how to teach them that this love is found between people who respond to a sense of romantic ethics and not between those who respond to moral customs.

The most obedient of these women depend on the gazes of those who love them: to be as they are, they need the approval, the consent and the permission of those relatives close to them, especially their mothers, their friends and their romantic partners. They seek to know that they are not wrong in the judgments of those who cannot evaluate them because they don't understand who these women are, how they are, nor why these women are as they are.

The most rebellious try to convince themselves that they don't need anyone's approval. They have known since they were little that they do not love as they ought: they never stop thinking. But they also know that they love: they never stop feeling.

They doubt the forms of their love, but they don't doubt their romantic motivations: they know that because they are strong they can be good, even though they don't know how to explain themselves and even though their loved ones do not understand them, given that sometimes they seem too rational and hard and other times too temperamental or sensitive. Some decide to run the risk of showing themselves as they are during childhood, before their parents—they let out into the open the storm of emotions and thoughts ravaging their insides. Others wait until they are adults, when they discover that, even in those moments when they feel that they have lost everything, they are still eager to learn. They are prepared to tolerate the aggression, suffering, and inevitable wounds that will follow in the wake of their showing their wildness in a domesticated world, because they trust that they are neither completely crazy nor utterly sick. And even though they've relied on nearly imperceptible signs, they believe that the precise embrace, one able to understand them, able to calm their anxieties, exists in reality.

Instead of feeling out of place, they opt not to fit in and to escape from all romantic models already in place among women of their generation.

They accept their emotional syncretism. They translate their emotional bilingualism, so that rather than living in a world of *neither/nor* they live in a world of *both/and*. They reconcile themselves to the fact that they have always loved differently: they have always needed true love more than life itself, but they don't need love in order to live truly.

In an article published in the 1920s, the iconoclastic Argentine writer *par excellence*, Roberto Arlt, answered a reader who had asked him 'in what way one should live in order to be happy': "I think that there is a way to live in relation to others and to oneself that, if it does not confer happiness, gives to the individual who practices it a kind of magical power over others: it's sincerity. To be sincere with everyone, even though it turns people against you. Even though your soul breaks against obstacles. Even though you are left alone, isolated and bleeding. This is not a formula for a happy life, but it is a way of developing strength and of examining life's content, of looking below that surface which constantly nauseates and tricks us."

Paula, Natasha, Alessandra, Michelle, Andrea, Laurie and other women like them appear to follow the letter of this law with great precision. They don't know what is happening to them, emotionally, but they know that to understand themselves, they must use heretofore unknown criteria of happiness and justice in romantic relationships.

They stop blaming themselves and they stop blaming others: no one is to blame for the fact that they were born feeling too wild to fit into social conventions. But they recognize that it is their responsibility to decide if they prefer to keep living in the jungle, hidden in their secret spaces, renouncing forever their hope of being understood by those by whom they wish to be loved; if they choose to live in captivity because they fear themselves too much, because they let themselves be cared for by those who love them without understanding them; or if they are ready to develop the strength to learn—to invent, discover, create—a system that would let them move freely between their syncretically savage ways of loving and the dissociated, contradictory, and incomplete, but comprehensible and recognizable, civilized ways of loving.

If they opt for this last possibility, they accept the fact that they must be the first to open a dialogue: they must translate themselves and find simple, specific and precise words with which to explain to us their feelings and thoughts. They must make an effort not to resort to the screams of pain and rage that escape them whenever they feel misunderstood.

They are the first to give themselves over to a precise embrace: they keep with rigorous prolixity, and make explicit with total transparency, their emotional syncretisms because they trust that they will avoid some of the many possible miss-encounters— those not generated by lack of love but by misunderstandings.

Despite the pain, the fear of being wrong and the discomfort of feeling different, some women my daughters' age follow Arlt, who insisted: "Don't look at what others are doing. Don't be bothered a bit by the opinion of anyone near you. Be yourself, yourself over all, instead of being good or bad, instead of feeling pleasure or pain, instead of choosing life or death." They may not even have heard the name of this author, but they appear more than ready to obey his proposals rather than continuing to be good in the socially mandated sense.

Tired of so many romantic disillusions, perplexed by feeling so lost in the romantic terrain when they are so successful otherwise, they decide to use, in order to leave this *terra incognita*, the same resources with which they would try to escape a professional, social or cultural confusion. They decide to forget everything they've learned, to be emotional autodidacts, to dedicate themselves to the discovery, creation and invention of their own definitions of the best love, of their own romantic models. They wrest from their parents' teachings the best and most useful information, giving it new settings and therefore new meanings. They throw themselves into the task, helping themselves with their recognized abilities: intelligence, obstinacy, tenacity, valor, honesty and dedication to their desires, the ability to overcome problems and to learn from their mistakes.

They have certain difficulties teaching themselves and learning how to be patient with themselves and with their partners, as this quality—so important for an apprenticeship that does not rely on tested recipes or on steps to follow that promise success—does not form part of the usual panoply of virtues of women my daughters' age. *They throw themselves down the well*—in a gloss by Arlt—trying to understand which are their romantic mistakes and which their emotional equivocations. Because they seem to know, as does Arlt, that making mistakes is an inevitable part of the apprenticeship process: "One makes mistakes when one must make mistakes. Not a minute before or a minute after. Why? Because such is what life has ordered, life this mysterious force. If you have made a mistake while acting sincerely it will be pardoned. Or it will not be pardoned. It doesn't matter. You follow your path. Against wind and tide. Against everyone, if that is necessary. And believe me: there will come a moment in which you feel so strong that life and death will become two playthings in your hands." The women do not know if this last is true, but they do know that, if they know themselves more, if they understand themselves better, they will stop fearing themselves. For this reason, they do not skimp in their efforts to understand which aspects of themselves are lovable and which unlovable, why they deserve to be loved and why feared, when and how they request embraces, when and how they offer embraces to others.

And they know that many of the romantic miss-encounters happen because emotionally contradictory people do not look at life with the same binocular vision as these women; emotionally contradictory people do not think and feel at once, are not strong and good at once.

These women discover that, if they are not satisfied with the happiness offered by the worlds of power or love, if they're prepared to create their own romantic system, based on love of truth, and to look for those who wish to inhabit this new world with them, then they must sustain 'against wind and tide' their own ways of loving, even if they appear strange and incomprehensible misfits. To be able to explain themselves to the other, they must understand themselves better.

Women who feel everything believe that they feel nothing; they are afraid that they are no one, while knowing too much. They know that every human being is alone, is born and dies alone, a world unto itself, an isolated island, a point of view, a speck in the infinite universe. And they need a love that offers them the possibility of tolerating this knowledge.

They need an embrace that helps them integrate into a harmonious whole the little fragments of their dispersed affects, their multiple *I*s, that helps them bear existential solitude and the finite quality of the body. For them, true love is that which conjoins the sacred and the profane, the social and the personal, the eternal and the ephemeral, the soul and the body, the person and the partnership; it is that which knits together, into a precisely measured fabric, the masculine and the feminine, strength and goodness. It is that which lets them love themselves.

I return to Laurie's story: "The day I met a man as complex as myself I felt rejection of him. It was like hearing my answering machine message and wanting to turn off the machine because my voice sounded so strange. I didn't go home thinking I'd met someone like myself, but thinking, like my mother, about how atypical, contrarians and unstable this man would be. But when I told my mother why I didn't like him, she began to praise him for the same things I thought she would reject. I began to cry. If she accepted him as he was, that meant that she accepted me as I was. When she advised me to go after him, I felt that I had acquired for the first time the liberty to choose for myself. It was as if I'd broken through the last brick in the wall that had prevented us from seeing each other and from embracing each other. I understood that it didn't matter whether or not my mother understood every aspect of myself or whether or not I fit into her molds. It was enough to know that each fit into the other's embrace."

The fact, however, is not that Laurie's mother has accepted her as she is. What happened is that Laurie, tolerating exclusions, solitudes, emotional miss-fittings and miss-encounters, has accepted herself and shown her mother that it is not necessary to be the same as the other in order to accept her. Laurie knew how to show her mother that it is necessary merely to be precise in the knowledge and acceptance of differences.

If we mothers learned from our daughters' new ways of loving, we would also escape from vicious circles of emotional contradiction. If our daughters' romantic partners learned how to dance the choreographies of shared loves, they too would escape the lacerations of divided loves.

"One night mom and dad tried to explain to me why I had to finish school, why I had to have a particular degree even though later I would work in another field entirely. They didn't know what to do with me. While they talked, I imagined that he was an eggplant smoking a pipe and she was a squash with spectacles," one of these women remembers. "They wanted me to acquire some social identity. They wanted me to be something; anything would do, but someone with status. But I wasn't ready to disguise myself as *anyone* merely to cover up my existential nudity. I was very upset when I realized that they wouldn't understand me if I tried to explain this. That night I sobbed until they came to comfort me and then I was calm again: I had cried all a person could cry. That was all I needed: that they hold me, that they make me feel, even for an instant, that we were not alone in the immensity of space. That, for me, is love."

Some women my daughters' age discover that the human condition of being alone does not oblige them to go through life alone, separated or isolated from other human beings. They manage to disentangle their knotted emotions and to discover, finally, what true love is for them: such love is that which allows them to embrace in a way that lets them feel at home, that sustains them in the face of existential solitude, the end of life, the certainty of death and the abysm of difference. They no longer seek a grandiose or complete embrace, but one ready to make an effort to decode and to help them to decode their complex emotional needs. And, consequent upon their commitment to truth, they offer to their loved ones the same embrace they request from them.

10

Joint Loves

"If I am not for myself, who will be for me? If I am only for myself, what am I?" teaches old Talmudic wisdom.

My daughters and some of their peers have a hard time being for themselves; the other interests them too much for them to be able to separate themselves from others' gazes. And so they seek something more than what Walter Benjamin describes as happiness, "the possibility to perceive oneself without fear." They also wish to be perceived without fear by those by whom they wish to be loved. More, they aspire to be understood, cared for, nurtured, consoled, nourished and embraced by those who love them in that intimate space in which they fear themselves and where their internal angels and devils engage in constant and evenly matched battles.

My daughters and some of their peers long to maintain love relationships in which the *I* that is *for themselves* coincides with the *I* that is also *for others*.

In order for the other to love them as they are—and, consequently, for them to understand better their own rarities, to correct their faults and to perfect their virtues—these women discover that they must unlearn the ways of loving and of naming love they learned from their mothers.

They question the contradictory emotional system they saw us inhabiting: they decide to abandon the two territories of divided loves and to finish their interminable wandering between the two. They trust that, in this way, they will manage to escape the vicious circles of rage and blame, of victims and victors, of submissions and rebellions, of emotional miss-encounters and misunderstandings.

Some invented new ways of loving when they were little and had barely begun to relate to others. They seem to have understood from birth the profound significance of Prophet Hillel's phrase: if they are not for themselves, no one will be. And, at once, they also seem to have known since birth that to be only for themselves robs their lives of meaning.

In the revision of emotional accountabilities that has marked their identities since childhood, they try to be as just and compassionate with themselves as with others. Paula taught me this in October 1995, when she wrote to me from the Luxembourg Gardens, where she found herself resting during a vital pilgrimage that had brought her to the streets of Paris:

"Hi, mom and life companion:

Today I found some roses the color of tea, those you like so much, and I felt that you were as present to me, as with me, as those roses. I know our last phone conversation was ugly. Sorry for having yelled at you when I couldn't take any more of your endless recommendations and constant corrections. Let's not become desperate, please. I know that we both want what's best for me. I know that we both seek cleanness and clarity in our actions and our relationships. I know, too, that you lack confidence in me and I think it's because you lack confidence in your way of being a mother. You torment yourself with what you never told me, without realizing that what you did teach me was that trusting in the vagaries of life is our way of looking for a true form of being in the world. It's very easy to be together when my way of being coincides with yours or when I do what you want, but it's harder to remember that we love each other when we differ. I ask that you trust the essence of each of us and that you remember that every life has its own shape.

Please, love me more lightly. I don't ask you to be more superficial or more banal or disinterested in your way of loving but that you give less importance to the details in which we differ and trust more in our shared values, values you taught me. The future is the future and it gestates in the present. You gave me life but now my life is my own and it's me who builds it. Know that my inner compass comes from that voice which whispers inside me and which teaches me much more than the screams with which you scold me or the silences with which you punish me. The shortest path between two human beings who love one another is possibility, even though this is not the straight easy line we imagine it to be.

Your life companion and daughter who loves you,

Paula".

Paula has always questioned my imprecise embraces, my divided loves, my dichotomous sentiments. In this letter she asked me to liberate her from the weight of an embrace that she didn't need with the same intensity as when, during her childhood, she clamored for an embrace then absent. Paula asked my forgiveness for having yelled at me, but this moment of anger, like the others, was motivated by love. She questioned my embraces knowing that we could embrace each other more fully and more clearly.

Women like her need to abandon feelings of rage and blame even when these are the only affects understood by those who are unlike them. In some cases, the painful truth is that some mothers and some men reject these women because, failing to understand them and so fearing them, they are not prepared to exercise the emotional precision these women need. But there are other mothers and other men who wish to understand. If these women trusted themselves more, if they had the courage to speak from within their emotional truths, if they decided to show themselves to others as they know themselves to be inside, if they allowed themselves to be as they are, without being so dependent on the other's likes or preferences, and if they stopped fearing themselves and fearing the other, they would help the other to be less afraid of himself. They would be able to tell when the other was truly dangerous and when he was merely confused in his complexity.

For emotional syncretes, love doesn't consist of giving themselves over as prey to the best hunter or turning themselves into the most powerful hunter of other prey. Instead, love consists of not having to defend themselves from misunderstandings nor having to argue to make themselves heard. It consists in understanding themselves and being understood as they are: their affects are difficult, but not impossible, to decode. They trust that they can understand—and make understand those who love them—that their emotional needs are complex, but not always confused; they are intricate, but not always impossible to disentangle; they are surprising, but not always bizarre.

They seek to dance a love choreography based in respect and trust, not in admiration or idealization. It requires the understanding of the soul more than a corporeal embrace, tender lucidity more than passionate blindness, mutual enrichment stemming from differences more than a summary of similarities. People who dare dance this love privilege general emotional agreement and do not fear specific disagreements. To the contrary: they begin from the necessity of thinking, feeling and existing as separate beings who love one another. They don't seek someone who knows all the answers, but someone who permits them all questions: always changeful, always energetic, always after the truest truth in a world where everything is relative. Moreover, they look for a romantic embrace that will help them to formulate, better than they do at present, the sometimes confusing and disorganized interrogations with which they regard themselves. They seek a dance companion who respects them—and why not say it, who understands them—even more than what they respect and understand themselves; they need an embrace that will tolerate all the questions, even those they fear to ask themselves.

Some women my daughters' age throw themselves into their romantic searches with more confidence than others. They have to deal with mothers who don't understand them entirely but who try to respect them: they are at peace with us and with themselves. Others abandon their resentments and make peace with their mothers: they understand why their mothers hurt them. They understand that their mothers wished to comprehend them but lacked the necessary tools to be able to do so. They grieve as much for their mothers' emotional impotencies as for their own lacks of emotionally competent mothers.

Still others abandon whatever hopes they may have had of obtaining their mothers' embrace and make peace that way. They understand why they feel so hurt. They understand that their mothers possess the tools to be able to understand them but do not wish to use them: they are not prepared to lose emotional control learning new ways of loving, for them as yet unknown. The emotional accounts of these women indicate that, to trust in love, they must distance themselves definitively from maternal affects. With pain, they accept that there are loves that kill and that, to save themselves, they need separations that cure. Otherwise, their fear of themselves will only increase as they see that even their own mothers are frightened when they show themselves as they are.

They receive from their mothers an active stimulus, a silent permission, an affectionate but insensitive look or a devastating absence of recognition. And then they begin the work of unlearning the contradictory forms of love, discovering, in the process of seeking another emotional truth: they recognize themselves as women who love strangely, but who do love. They begin to express with precision who they are and what they need. They find new words to define their ways of feeling.

Those who believe that truth will bring them closer to happiness are not prepared to content themselves with a love that is only thought or felt, only distrusted or credited, only free or secure, only sexual or companionate, only impassioned or tender, only traditional or rebellious, only true in parts. Those who believe that truth will bring them closer to happiness also resist choosing between loving and being loved, being a desiring subject and a desired object, being strong or good, being rewarded for love or power. They know that split partial loves, though they may seduce with offers of total truths and total embraces, only bring partial truths and partial happiness. These women do not want to win any emotional contest, they know that they do not need the best love—the most recognized, publicized or disputed—but the precise embrace, that lets them reconcile between themselves and their angels and devils, which in turn are reconciled to each other.

They reach their destination by understanding who they truly are. And they understand that they are not—and do not wish to be—a negotiation between two ways of being such as that which defines their mothers' contradictory emotional identities. Their love relationships are not a constant suturing of ruptured feelings, not a constant piecing together of people broken through power struggles. They do not want a passion born from the fear of losing the loved one, but rather the happiness produced by the certainty of mutual recognition.

Emotional syncretes who do the work necessary for self-understanding know that they are not the result of a mixture or of a compromise between contradictory emotions. And neither is this the kind of love they seek. They accept that they are strange, but they do not accept being considered sick. They know that they are paradoxical, but they try to avoid being contradictory. They recognize how demanding they can be, but they refuse to be called insatiable. They defend their multiple emotional interests because they know of the richness of such interests and trust that they can satisfy some of their desires that, while appearing dispersed and ambiguous, are multifaceted and diverse.

These women know that they feel different, not only from their mothers but also from 98% of their peers—as Laurie said—

but they no longer wish to hide who they are or how they feel. They want to belong to their communities without impoverishing fragmentations, negotiations or evasions. To make themselves be understood as they are, they are ready to confront the patient work of trying to understand themselves.

And in the emotions, as in life, something exists once it can be named, one can understand once one can find the exact word, once the something stops being merely "a pulse that beats in the dark," as Celaya says.

Women my daughters' age stop navigating between two contradictory ideologies of love once they manage to invent, create, discover or find new ways of naming their emotional needs. When they can express, without fear or rage, their feelings. When they are able to laugh at themselves and at their mothers and partners, when they share with them a sincere and transparent embrace.

Because emotional syncretes don't want to admire or be admired: they want a love based on mutual respect. They neither ask for nor offer an obligatory love or an asphyxiating hug; neither do they propose a return to the traditional loves of the past, to a time when women were economically subsumed under patriarchal power. They are not prepared to behave (nor do they expect their mothers or partners to behave) as if they were only good, obedient, dependent, always ready to do what the other wants. They do not tolerate the idea of marrying for the long haul if this means routinely repeating loving gestures out of obligation, or from fear of being scolded or punished, or based on submission to a moral imperative. They are independent enough not to need the constant (and sometimes burdensome) presence of the loved one. But neither do they want to behave (nor do they expect their mothers or partners to behave) as if they were only strong, rebellious, limited to their own desires. They don't want to be prisoners of a regimented emotional life, but neither do they want to be nomads hunting constantly for slippery emotions.

Unlike many of their peers and unlike their mothers, emotional syncretes don't debate between submission to and rejection of family ties. They want to marry—in a daily way that, incrementally, forms the long term—those whom they love and to choose, freely and fully, each daily loving gesture. They are dependent enough to need the unconditional (if not unlimited) presence of the loved one.

For these women, choreographies of love do not obey prefabricated obligations nor fixed orders. But neither do they obey the irresponsible, unforeseen or arbitrary orders that follow from uncontrollable emotional impulses. These women discover that, while trying to avoid the suffering caused by their mothers' and peers' emotional contradictions, they have become lost and entangled in emotional labyrinths. Enclosed there, often encapsulated and hidden, they discover that the keys to their strange ways of loving are not found in either one of the partial divided ways of loving, but in the interstices between both:

1. *Between dependence and independence, they discover emotional autonomy.*

Some women discover that autonomy—"the condition of following one's own laws and making decisions on one's own," according to the dictionary—lets them be both dependent and independent at once. In the process of such discovery, they give new meanings to both terms.

In dependent relationships, both merits and faults are the patrimony of the other: it's the mother's fault or to her credit if her baby fattens up or not. In independent relationships, both merits and faults are always one's own doing: it's the baby's fault or to her credit if she fattens up or not. In autonomous relationships, merits and faults influence each other proportionally: the baby fattens up or not based on a complex relationship between the two. Maybe the baby doesn't fatten up because she doesn't want to or can't feed herself or because the mother doesn't want to or can't feed her. Maybe the baby fattens up thanks to a cycle created by a combination of goods: the baby wants to and can feed herself and the mother wants to and can feed the baby. Or maybe the baby doesn't fatten up because of a cycle created by a combination of problems: the baby doesn't want to or can't feed herself and the mother doesn't want to or can't feed the baby. If the milk is abundant but the baby doesn't suckle, the baby will not grow. If the milk is scarce, the baby will not grow no matter how strongly she suckles. If the mother and baby articulate their capacities and needs, they will find a way for the milk to reach its destination, to the satisfaction of both; if they don't relate to one another as autonomous interdependent organisms, it's inevitable that one of them will remain unsatisfied.

Sometimes, women who have sought autonomy since they were little believe that they are not lovable because their mothers didn't love them; others, because their mothers don't know how to love. But when they leave behind dichotomous paradigms that divide the world into dependent victims and independent victors, they discover that they feel neither loved nor loving because both they and their mothers are prisoners of a negative relation created by both or by a moment superior to both. They realize that both are victors and victims at once, and in the free exercise of autonomy they try to liberate themselves from this negative dependence. If they succeed, they will also liberate their mothers from the role of victor-victim.

They reject relationships that demand obedience and privilege those that demand responsibility for one's own life. They don't want an independence that exposes them to solitude or to a lack of emotional belonging, but neither do they want a dependence that exposes them to submission or to violent confrontations with their loved ones. They affirm that they don't love their mothers because they need them (a need felt by weak sons and daughters) but that they need them because they love them. That is, they choose to depend because they know themselves to be independent. They decide freely in what way, how much and how to depend on their mothers. They are able to say no when they wish, an ability that lets them say yes when they wish. Because they know that they are strong in the emotional plane, they can be good there as well.

These women know that relationships between two independent people who choose to depend on each other can only be built upon a base of consensual and shared autonomy. One used to say to her mother: "I can fall asleep alone, but I like it better when you cuddle me until I fall asleep." So her mother learned to cuddle her for the pure pleasure of freely given love and not to consider the daughter's request capricious, different, whimsical. During her adolescence, this same woman privileged her own desire not to increase her mother's anxiety in a difficult moment by going on a mountain-climbing trip with friends. From a state of dependence, the daughter would have stayed home, angry with her suffocating mother. From a state of independence, the daughter would have gone away, and would have been made to feel guilty by her mother. From an autonomous state, the daughter knew that she was strong and maintained her personal desires, which knowledge permitted her to stay home because she was good and decided to do so—not because of her mother's emotional manipulations. In their relationships with men, these women seek to construct a joint love, whose base is the consensual decision to depend upon one another made by two autonomous beings, independently.

2. *Between fusion and individuation, they discover dialogue.*

Since they were little, some women have known that the static happiness of silence in which one listens to only one voice is not for them. Love for them consists of a reciprocal relationship of mutual constant apprenticeship between beings: the *I* and the *you* and the *we* conjoin in dialogue.

They know that reality is not entirely "what mother says," but that neither is it what they say: they know that reality appears in various guises depending on one's perspective. They are interested in understanding all of reality, that which integrates the viewpoints of distinct and complementary gazes. They also know that they can argue, accuse, and attack until they win, until one voice remains, defending their own points of view. But they are not interested in winning and imposing their wills on their mothers. They are not interested in losing and submitting to their mothers' wills. They want neither the silence of the vanquished nor that of the conquerors. They do not become silent in accusation or shout in domination and they don't want their mothers to do so either. They want to engage in dialogue with their mothers, to listen to them and to be listened to until they find the places of concord that will let them disagree without threat to either.

They don't expect from their mothers or partners the total complete embrace that would offer or ask for all answers. They know that such an embrace condemns one to monologue, whether of fusion or of individuation. They wish to dance a love choreography based in the dialogue between those who dare to learn from the other, to incorporate other points of view into their own, and to see a shared reality that includes the loved one's perspective. This dialogue only takes place between people who share the desire to be together and to embrace one another mutually, knowing that unconditional love recognizes the conditions under which each partner needs to be loved.

One of these women remembers that, during the long years of her refusal to eat consequent upon her mother's death, her maternal grandmother left at her disposal various dishes without requiring her to eat any of them. The granddaughter's way of maintaining dialogue was to let her grandmother know that she appreciated this care, and ate in secret, so that no one—not even she herself—would see that she wanted to live. After a time, she was able to cry for her mother in her grandmother's arms. Presently the woman accepts that her husband, an artist who needs solitude and silence for his creative work, may disappear without her knowing where he's gone, as long as he agrees to return at a time mutually agreed upon earlier. He understands that in facing each absence, his wife relives, in a small way, her fear of losing a loved one, as she lost her mother during her childhood. The unconditionality between both partners consists of mutual recognition of the individual needs of each, consented to in a dialogue that lets them perceive, precisely and in any moment, where each is located in the other's emotional terrain.

These women only feel understood, comforted and enriched by an embrace that recognizes, accepts and respects a certain distance between they and their loved ones. They want to look at and to be looked at by the loved one, but only from a distance that integrates the desire to be with the loved one with the knowledge of being a separate person.

Love for these women consists of the reciprocal surrender to individual intimacy, by means of dialogue, during the process of establishing a relation that lets them feel with relief the loved one's presence *despite*—or precisely *because*—they know that every human being is alone. Happiness for these women comes from feeling so much a part of the loved one that they can imagine existing as a single being, something that may take place only when they know themselves to be separate. Without such a dialogue, they feel abandoned or invaded. And for this reason they practice this unique embrace which tries to conjoin what is separate, this unique love which tries to transform contradictory monologues into paradoxical dialogues.

Women (and men) of my daughters' generation learned from their parents and from their societies that one cannot be and not be in a fixed way at the same time, that one cannot have and not have a certain quality. They learned that in the divided world in which we lived, there existed power or love, strength or goodness, final victory or final defeat. They learned that, in contradictions, one term necessarily and inevitably makes the other disappear.

But some women (and some men) of my daughters' generation incorporated the conjunction *and* into their vocabularies. They know that life is made of paradox. They know that sometimes being, thinking and feeling a certain way can be explained, justified or supported by the possibility of the same person's being, thinking and feeling another, apparently opposite way. They know that sometimes it's necessary to be far from or to take a certain distance from the loved one in order to be able to be close to and embrace that person with precision, and that they can only be good and capable of listening to the other because they are strong, capable of making themselves heard.

3. *Between the expected and the unexpected, they discover creativity.*

For these women, the ability to discover the extraordinary within the ordinary brings more interesting challenges than the ability to break up the monotony of the known with the excitement of the unknown. Everyday magic delights them, as does the possibility of finding more of it through an everyday practice of training, patience and rigor. They know that artistic creation is a strange combination of ten percent inspiration and ninety percent perspiration, of talent and work, and they act like artists in their own emotional lives. And so they manage to disobey the conventional sentiment that dictates the customs for those who feel defined definitively as good or bad or strong or weak; and so, too, do they elude oppositional definitions that would make them behave as marginalized, rebellious or contrarians in their emotional lives.

Since they were little, they have found more pleasure in inventing their own rituals than in repeating those of others, even if these are the latest word in romantic fashion. One of these women was the despair of her mother for rejecting the elaborate gifts designed to win her over, preferring to play with her grandmother's old buttons or with a simple set of colored pencils her father had given her. In addition, the daughter told the mother that she didn't want to be like her, as the latter didn't know how to enjoy herself unless she were being entertained by others' gifts or ideas. Today this woman is happily cultivating mutual delight with a man she's been with for more than ten years.

These women resist the consumption of novelties, the temptation of being fascinated by the sporadic contacts of a free erratic love. But they also resist repeating the immutable routines of a regimented bureaucratic love. They know that both systems propose to liberate them from emotional responsibilities, and they reject both solutions: they are not willing to let passion's enchantment or habit's weight reign over their feelings. The novelty born of a constant change of partner condemns one to nomadism, solitude and emotional miss-fitting: it stops love from growing beyond the moment of its own birth, from developing and fructifying. But the ritualized repetition of gestures that accompanies stability condemns one to immobility, petrifaction of feeling, emotional rigidity: it stops love from transforming, modifying and adjusting to the changing needs of the partners. These women know that strategies aimed at stopping time and maintaining love's freshness are destined to failure. More ambitious than their mothers and some of their peers, these women seek a love that maintains itself while changing and changes in order to maintain itself.

When they were little they showed their families how to recover as innovative artistic creations the familial rituals rejected or ignored by their mothers. While they refused to comply with hypocritical social obligations, they demanded that intimate encounters between family members be maintained. As adults they refuse to navigate between boredom and danger: they seek a partner more exciting, demanding and challenging than the conventional, but more secure, trustworthy and calming than the marginal. They guarantee the stability—not the annihilation—of a relationship by remaking it, without endangering it, constantly. They learn to eroticize tenderness: they bring together in daily life the epiphany of the encounter and the ecstasy of romantic discovery, with a known man in everyday places.

4. *Between politeness and frankness, they discover respect.*

They want to be good, affectionate; they want to live a nice life. They want to be strong, honest; they want to live an authentic life. The resolution of this contradiction is the most important challenge facing these women.

They have learned how to defend themselves, how to defend their ideas, desires and vital spaces since they were little. One of them still scares herself today, remembering how as a teenager she yelled at her mother: "If you interfere with my life, I'll kill you." The fear of disappearing by doing what the other wants is as strong as the fear of feeling egotistical or intransigent—bad—if they do as they wish. Years later, this same daughter realized: "suffering, I learned how much I harmed myself by using my mother in order to fight my own demons." Since they were little, these women have danced with their mothers a contradictory emotional choreography, which goes from submission to violence, from rage to blame, from hatred of their mothers to hatred of themselves.

They react defensively to any comment that strikes them as critical, adverse or authoritarian. As if they lacked the ability to choose, the first response that escapes them, spontaneously and without thought, is *no*. But they don't always wish to reject what their mother or partner suggests. Sometimes they want to say *yes* and to rest in the arms, decisions and care of those who love them. Perhaps their mothers and societies so encouraged them to be strong that they are condemned to *always* be strong. But the transformation of contradictions and confusions into paradoxes and complexities lets them exercise a new way of feeling. These women learn that, to cure themselves of their addiction to combat, to a permanent defensive attitude, they need to respect themselves, to consider their own weaknesses, to listen to their various feelings, desires and needs, and not only to those impelling them to be strong.

They appear to have been born efficient, able of arranging their lives without help, or doubt. Their mothers became used to not paying them too much attention: these daughters seemed not to need them, they solved their own problems better than anyone else. They themselves became used to not needing their mothers in order to live. However, this did not mean that they did not need love. How to understand that the same daughter who threatened her mother with death in order to escape her advice was also desperate for her mother's embrace? Neither her mother nor she understood that she needed a simple gesture of maternal affection, not a demonstration of excellent pedagogy. Neither her mother nor she understood that exercising the right to live in truth and only in truth didn't mean that she would not need tenderness, pity and compassion to be able to tolerate the intermittent pain of such a way of life.

Some women learned to listen to, recognize and respect their fears, their pains, their anguish, their needs for tenderness and affection. Their self-respect let them respect the other. They practiced tenderness that were not based in sorrow and discussions that were not based in argument, because for them loving acts are not born from weakness, nor debate from a show of strength or competition.

Paula asked me to caress her, sitting in front of the television, simply because she wanted affection. It was hard for me to understand that she was not weak for making this request. Years later I understood that it was only due to her great strength that she could tell me honestly that, despite not liking my way of loving her, she needed my love.

She and others like her overcame the emotional contradictions they learned from their mothers and practice respect in their relationships. They are polite and honest at once, and they demand reciprocity from their partners.

5. *Between relaxation and exhilaration, they discover eagerness to learn.*

The apprenticeship begins with vertigo, when novelty's splendor draws their attention, and continues in a slow rhythm as they familiarize themselves with the unknown. These women share an exuberant enthusiasm when faced with all types of novelties discovered in every moment, but they also share the tenacity required to unravel the enigmas of the unknown, to learn from them and to appropriate their riches. Because they are curious, their minds need 'new nourishment every day,' as one phrases it; because they are demanding, they are not content with swallowing and expulsing the novelty in an act of compulsive consumption. They want to know, to metabolize, to get rid of what does not suit them and to keep what nourishes them. They want to reproduce this nourishment whenever they wish, to avoid the temptation of devouring it all at once and losing it as a consequence. They share both enthusiasm for feeding themselves novelties and tenacity for dominating the impatience that would hinder the digestion of such.

They have, since they were little, criticized their mothers for being content with anything less than excellence. I was one of those mothers criticized for wanting to know without making the effort to learn.

When we celebrated Natasha's fifteenth birthday, we had just moved back to Buenos Aires, but we came full of the Brazilian festive rituals we had learned during our ten years in Rio de Janeiro. We prepared with enormous care the right foods; we decorated the house and picked out the music, the games and the gifts we would give at the party's end. Then we waited for the guests. It was a long wait. After midnight, three of Natasha's forty classmates appeared, and they left very shortly. I cried, humiliated, failed, and scared. Natasha, despite her own anguish, consoled me by saying that my evaluative criteria had failed, that this mess showed that we did not understand the social codes of Buenos Aires. She maintained the tranquility necessary to learn and she developed an adaptation of her rituals to the customs of the new place. Today she organizes splendid parties in any city in which she has been living for a few months.

It was during that same period that, after having passed a certain class, she disconcerted me by asking to take private classes in the same subject. She said that she knew "for the exam" but that she was ignorant of *what* she knew; understanding was more important for her than having passed the exam. The teacher's positive evaluation and the legitimacy conferred by it were not enough for her, as they were for me. She wanted to test herself. She needed to be for herself as well as for others.

Today women like Natasha run the risk of confusing enthusiasm with voracity, patience with slowness. They know they should maintain constant alertness as much for the avoidance of false accusations of exaggerated tranquility in their partners as for the avoidance of accusations of exaggerated anxiety in themselves. They seek an embrace that permits them the curiosity and the tranquility needed to transform a taste for the new into a lasting apprenticeship in life.

6. *Between outer-directedness and inner-directedness, they seek justice.*

These women suffer when they are accused, unjustly, of being selfish. They seek emotional truth and find arbitrary generosity as dangerous as calculated manipulations. They believe that neither of these attitudes takes into account the other, nor bases itself on respect for the needs, desires and possibilities of the two people involved in the transaction. They believe in short that acts of arbitrary generosity or of calculated manipulation are acts not of love but of power.

One woman explains that, when she was little, her mother scolded her for not sharing her chocolates with her brother. She couldn't explain to her mother that she was not bad, avaricious or selfish for having saved her chocolates for a longer amount of time than did her brother. In fact, it struck the girl as unjust that she should have to make up with her own candy for her brother's voracity, lack of care or inefficiency. She recognized the scene of her relishing her chocolates in the face of her brother's lack as something ugly, disagreeable and almost violent. But she didn't understand why her mother couldn't see that forcing her to "feed a drone"—giving her candy to her jealous brother who was unable to regulate his appetites—was equally ugly, disagreeable and violent. How to leave this scene? How to create others in which wealth is shared? Which scene lets both participants in the emotional transaction act generously?

Some women think that flawless emotional accountability helps create such scenes of reciprocal and mutually convenient generosity.

"María Dolores is right to herself, but not right to everybody". Natasha was six years old when she defended her point of view, combating mine with the same strength with which I tried to explain that she had behaved very badly towards a friend. I maintained that María Dolores had "all the right in the world" to be mad at Natasha, who insisted that each girl had all her own right to be mad at the other, and thereby questioned the criteria by which I judged justice. She didn't want to owe or to give less than her due, but neither did she want to be owed or to receive less than her due. She was pleased to share her toys with her friend, because in this way she discovered and learned new ways of playing, but she refused to accept that her friend would not share with her. It was difficult for me to avoid the "don't be bad" that escaped me, an echo of my mother's "be good" which I had heard so many times when I was my daughter's age.

But if my mother's "be good" had stimulated me to show myself as friendlier, making grow that desirable quality in my identity, my "don't be bad" tried to instigate in my daughter a show of being less disagreeable, making disappear from her identity that feared quality. My mother said: "Be more like that generous good Susana, and I will love you more." I said to my daughter: "Be less like that selfish bad Natasha and I will love you more." But my mother also insisted: "Be less like that weak Susana who doesn't do what's good for her and I will admire you more." And I in my turn insisted: "Be more like that strong Natasha who does what is best for her and I will love you more." Some women of my generation love contradictorily because we didn't know how to disentangle the emotional confusions caused us by our mother's incoherent messages. But Natasha and others like her have managed this feat: they have transformed emotional contradictions into paradoxes. They have learned that only because they are strong can they be good, and they seek relationships in which it is to both people's benefit to be generous with the other.

Their desire to be generous excludes the use of the victim's weapons: reclamation, complaint, accusations of abuse of power.

Similarly, their desire for healthy relationships excludes the use of the victor's arms: arbitrariness, threat, humiliating disqualification. Only reciprocal relationships permit them to stop mistrusting or calculating, defending or attacking. This reciprocity requires flawless accountability, which would guarantee generosity and healthfulness and avoid feelings of being taken advantage of (on the one side) or of being accused of speculation (on the other.) Such reciprocity also requires transparency in actions: each participant must know and make known to the other, with precise flawlessness, what is gained and what lost, what is at risk and how to protect from risk, what is offered and what asked for in each moment of every exchange.

7. *Between pragmatism and realism, they discover lucidity.*

As long as they don't find the right name for their strange feelings, strong women who wish to be good feel awkward, almost monstrous in their ways of expressing their feelings. They feel stupid when they say "I love you;" violent when they say "I don't like how you love me;" ingenuous when they suggest "let's try to love each other as we need to be loved;" skeptical when they confirm "we don't love each other as we need to be loved." They stay in an emotional limbo and hide their feelings out of fear of their own eccentricity. They believe that they know neither how to love nor how to be loved.

Since they were little, they have cried, laughed, been scared or brave in moments other than those that elicit these reactions from other people. They are not like the other girls. In some ways they are much easier to raise: they take care of themselves and we, their mothers, don't have to worry about whether they've done their homework, cleaned their rooms, or looked after their siblings. In other ways, they are much more difficult to raise: we don't understand their requests for love or their demonstrations of love because these strike us as incongruent with their intellectual capacities. At times they seem very adult and at others very infantile.

Not understanding them, very often we reject the embrace they offer us or do not give them the embrace they request. We criticize them, trying to format them to love as we believe one ought to love. But we don't understand that their oddities don't stem from emotional rebellions, behavioral problems, emotional illnesses or learning disabilities: their oddities express a different way of loving that, when misunderstood, transforms itself into anguish or anger, into blame or attack, into cold indifference or exaggerated neediness.

They have known since they were little that goodness in the world of love and strength in the world of power are finite qualities. They know with certainty that solitude is an inevitable part of human existence; that even the most perfect embrace disappears with the death of one of the people embracing. They accept— even before acceding to conceptual language—that human existence is finite, ephemeral and limited and that after birth no one ever fully enters another's embrace.

They have known since they were little that no two people are identical: every one has his own unique way of being, and so each embrace has its own size, scent, color, taste and texture. They know that people neither think nor feel in the same way, and that everything depends on the lens through which one looks at things. They know that one can never understand the other entirely, given that no one is identical to anyone else, given that no one speaks the exact same emotional language as the other.

They were born realists, but also idealists: they trust that human beings can create new realities, build bridges to join what is separated, cover immeasurable distances moved by their desire to broaden their horizons, see beyond a landscape that only allows a single perspective. One woman remembers a scene of love that struck her in its illumination of these two aspects of herself: "Every night, my grandfather put me to sleep by telling me stories. One time, because I hadn't fallen asleep, I asked him for more stories, and more and more, until he opened his mouth like he was going to begin another story but he was silent and then he laughed. I realized that he couldn't think of anything. I wasn't frustrated or angry, I didn't cry: I began to laugh too and I felt flooded with love. I'd never felt such connection in my life. I'd never felt so loved as I did that night, by my grandfather, who told me at the same moment that he wanted to satisfy me but couldn't. If a man made me feel that love, I would be his forever."

The dictionary defines lucid thus: "a person who acts with clarity, grace, liberality and elegance." Such is how some women act as they go about the task of transforming their romantic ideals into realities. Their lucidity conjoins their ways of being idealistic and realistic, romantic and pragmatic at once. Feeling and thinking, these women undertake the creation of a complex paradoxical relationship that is at the same time coherent and comprehensible: in brief, a joint love.

In his response to the reader who wanted to know how to love happily, Arlt added: "Soon, you will discover something that is not happiness but its equivalent: emotion. The terrible emotion of risking one's life and one's happiness. Not by playing cards, but by converting yourself into a kind of sentient human card who seeks happiness by means of the most extraordinary and unlooked-for combinations. Look, friend: make a base of sincerity for yourself and on this tightrope, with your truth in hand, cross life's chasm and triumph. No one, absolutely no one, can make you fall. And even those who today throw stones at you will come close to you tomorrow, smiling timidly. Believe this, friend: a sincere man is so strong that he is the only one who can laugh at everything and empathize with everyone."

11

THE PRECISE EMBRACE

In an interview, the actress Diane Lane notes that she was startled by the combination of intensity and naturalness she witnessed while watching a tango in Buenos Aires. "The tango is so dramatic, and the dancers feel so comfortable. There's no effort. It's extraordinary. It's like watching a bullfight in which the animal does not die." Lane continues by saying that she didn't try to dance because in tango it's necessary to "know how not to be left behind and to anticipate the steps: one can hurt oneself if one does not know what one is doing."

Natasha and Carlos, her husband, know very well what Lane is describing. And so, even though their lives are full of professional, social, community and family commitments, their Tuesday nights in Toronto are sacred: they never miss a tango class. For them, this activity is not merely about the enjoyment of the music and of the movement; it also constitutes the model of joint love they wish to build as a couple. They are as dedicated to finding the naturalness in such a dramatic dance, to moving brilliantly without hurting the other, to finding themselves in a common space for the steps, as they are to learning how not to hurt one another dancing the romantic choreography that sustains the precise embrace.

The love choreography of this embrace has, for strong good women, all the tension of a difficult and definitive bullfight. But this tension can be enjoyable and pleasurable for spectators and participants. Well danced, this romantic bullfight ends well: the dancers don't kill each other. Instead, the members of every good couple, each one both bull and bull fighter, regard each other, caress each other and calm each other where each hurts most, where each was hurt in previous fights, too awkward or too sanguine in their romantic eagerness.

Natasha and others like her—emotional syncretes who have taken the time to and done the work of decoding their ways of feeling—already know that they want to dance a love choreography so intense and—at the same time and with the same intensity—so natural as that tango which impressed Lane.

And what love will sate their emotional hunger? The precise embrace: that which calms their existential anguish in the exact way needed by each; it is that which says, in the specific language able to be understood by the listener, that one can live with the knowledge of death, understanding the whole of life while seeing its limits. The precise embrace is that which provides accompaniment to those who know, unequivocally, that we are all alone. And above all, the precise embrace is that which is not frightened by the paradoxical feelings, the multifaceted characters, the complex desires that comprise the world of these strong good women who are in the process of learning how to translate between their own languages and the languages of the world outside. The precise embrace is that which, knowing the beauty trapped within them, helps them to untangle, understand and conjugate into an intelligible form their encoded desires.

The precise embrace is not the best for everybody, but the perfect one for these women. Some of these women find it when still young; some others after rigorous introspective work, a hurting and long succession of trials and errors: there is no instruction manual that may help them understand and decipher their emotional syncretism, nor a map that will indicate them how to reach the longed for treasure.

Now, they seek a companion who understands that confrontations between those who accept differences celebrate life, while face-offs between those who don't tolerate differences summons death. But they also know that those who aspire to dance in this way need to learn how to control the stimulating strength enclosed in the savage desires of their little devils, making sure not to domesticate them too much. At the same time, they need to learn how to liberate the authentic goodness suffocated by the stifling obligations of their little angels, making sure not to turn them indifferent or irresponsible.

They know too that they must accomplish the first part of these tasks alone. They understand that, before beginning to practice this new romantic choreography, they must learn how not to be carried away by rage when they are not loved as they wish, how not to be carried away by guilt when they don't love as they believe they ought. Because love of truth has its own difficulties: if the dancers are not sufficiently protected against romantic mistrust, they can become infected by it and love while suffering from ingenuity and suspicion. Emotional syncretes tend to repeat their historical reactions: they hide in limbo and they act as if they are weak or bad, although they are not, if they feel rejected or misunderstood in their emotional expressions. To avoid the reopening of wounds of doubt, solitude or incomprehension, these women need to learn how to decipher whether the misunderstandings that inevitably arise during the process of learning this love are due to intentional cruelty, lack of sufficient information or simple communication problems.

To prevent this backsliding, the constant learning of a dance of provocative love requires a complement: the constant learning of the teachings of confrontational love.

At this point, the emotional syncretes are prepared to venture themselves in the complex choreographies of love danced by two. As in tango.

One of the most visible traits of this dance is that protagonism resides in the couple as a couple. Unlike other social dances, tango does not only follow the music but also develops its own inner logic based less on established steps and more on improvisation.

As Lane observed, in tango it is impossible to lag behind or to ignore future steps. One of the dancers begins the step and the other completes it, resulting in a sequence greater than the sum of its parts. Each dancer already knows that he can dance brilliant solos and marvelous duets. And so each wants something more: they are excited by the challenge of seeing if they also know how to dance a joint love, a dance of perfect connection with the partner, as exists in tango.

"No dance opposes domination like tango," says Richard Martin in *El tango sempiterno*, an essay collected by Simon Collier in his anthology *¡Tango!* According to Martin, tango offers "a new expression of masculine and feminine *bravados* and tenderness." In a similar way, strong and good people that seek to construct a love relationship that will deliver them the precise embrace know that, in this love choreography, the protagonism does not lie in one of its parts but on the couple. This love requires the conversion of competitive strength, which teaches that one must be and have the best of everything in everything, into cooperative force, which teaches how to live with excellence: constructing complex human relationships as precious valued works of art.

Let us imagine how one of these women moves in the terrain of the emotions.

She walks without hurry or anxiety: she does not expect to arrive anywhere, but to be there where she finds herself. She is alone amidst the tumultuous crowd of men and women radiating romantic happiness. She does not envy them—she knows that their happiness is not the one she wants. She thinks of the moment in which her own happiness will arrive.

She does not fear being marginal, a second-class citizen or sick or a failure: she no longer hides in partial, split loves or takes refuge in inconvenient loves. Her ways of loving have managed to emerge from limbo. As when the tango moved from the street to the salon, she began to practice the precise embrace in the forbidden slums of inconvenient loves. Having overcome the contradiction of split loves, she is ready to aspire to the practice of the precise embrace in more conventional social settings.

Finally she knows that she is hard to understand and that, in addition, she needs a love difficult to explain. Finally she feels comfortable in her own skin: she has learned that her emotional complexities can be explained by her enormous variety of emotional hues. After a long, painful and meticulous process of deciphering her emotions, she understands herself and loves herself as she is. She no longer looks for a man who will calm her existential anguishes, but for one who will share her way of looking at the world. She knows that the love she wants "can never be found by seeking, but that only those who seek can find it," as a Sufi proverb says.

Surprisingly, her gaze crosses paths with that of a man who seems interested in her. "When he sees how strange I am, will he stop looking?" she wonders, observing him with similar interest and cautious curiosity. But he doesn't stop looking, and she doesn't stop looking, and when both confirm their mutual interest, they slowly and softly draw closer to each other, avoiding the external influences that could rupture the magic of their nascent connection.

Let us arrest the scene's progress for a moment. Who is the man who recognizes the woman? What is the man like who doesn't look at other more familiar goods of women? In the majority of cases in which this encounter takes place and develops successfully, the man is also emotionally syncretic and also looks at life with a binocular vision. He is someone who, like her, thinks and feels at once. Someone who needs the freedom that comes from individuality and the security that comes from a strong sense of family belonging. Someone who never entirely surrenders himself and who always trusts completely. Someone who knows of death and celebrates life. Someone who knows incompleteness and believes in the precision of a romantic embrace. Someone who is, like her, at once strong and good in emotional terrain.

But, unlike her, this man has dedicated himself, since he was little, to trying not to seem strange. He has wanted so badly to be comforted by familial and social embraces that he has appeared to fit in completely to both. He may have discovered early that the fit was not as perfect as he thought and the adaptation only external: inside, in the limbo that only he knows exists as an important part of himself, he feels maladjusted, like a misfit, as strange as his strange companion. Or he may only have intuited the lack of proper fit: perhaps he has made such a strong effort to pass invisibly and not to be punished, persecuted or disqualified from his peers' romantic games that he does not even suspect that sometimes he acts as if he were bad and other times as if he were weak, even though he is neither, out of lack of conviction in the conveniences of a split love.

Because of these differences, he may be afraid of the woman to whom he is attracted, who may strike him as a little crazy; she may be afraid of the man who attracts her because he strikes her as a little oafish. If they overcome these barriers, they will see that they can draw close to each other without fear. Even better: with time they will discover that she is not unbalanced, but rather uses better than he the energies he keeps hidden; they will discover that he is not obsequious, but rather uses better than she stabilizing social connections. They can then win on all fronts: he, by reconnecting with his inner self, she, by reconnecting to the social world.

Maybe they understand immediately why they are attracted to each other; maybe it will take time for them to recognize each other. In any case, when their gazes cross, they intuit that they can build together a peaceful happiness. This happiness is not identical for each but it is equivalent: hers is due to the fact that she can finally be strong without running the risk of appearing bad and unfeminine; his is due to the fact that he can finally be good without running the risk of seeming weak and effeminate.

Silent, concentrated in thought and emotion, these strange beings prepare themselves for the ritual ceremony they have so hoped for: opening to the other the doors to their inner selves. They draw closer every moment: the time comes to choose how to dance. "I could stop calling her for a few days," he thinks. "I could use his best friend to make him jealous," she thinks. But both discard these and other strategies of conquest. They are not interested in winning in this way, they are not interested in scoring points off the other: "Either he knows and likes me as I am, or this story is no good for me," each thinks.

Both seek the same: they seek to give and get a precise embrace. In order to dance in a couple, they wish to meet a partner who detects the most intimate zone of the other's emotional being—this world of intricate emotions perceived by each with such ambivalence, sometimes like a treasure and sometimes like a sin—that which makes each who he is: beings strong but not bad, good but not weak. A partner who helps them to continue deciphering the complexities of their beings, who shares their emotional identity. Having made peace with their inner selves, emotional syncretes need the gaze of the other if they are to continue the work of disentangling their complexities. Like Alice, who falls in love with her husband all over again every time he calls her "adorably quirky," because he was the first to show her with this epithet that she was strange in the sense of being unique and not in the sense of being wrong. All their lives, emotional syncretes have heard what to them are incomprehensible accusations: they live in their own world, they are too complicated. The precise embrace of another syncrete lets them, finally, understand that their complex world is something special, desirable and needed by someone.

Finally they find themselves face to face and discover that, in joint love as in tango, neither is the other's mirror. If one moves the left foot, the other will move the left foot also—not the right, as a mirror image would do. The tango is danced with a light embrace that lets the dancers share a common axis, constituted for example by the dancers' right legs, while their left legs remain free to develop independent movements. Unlike other dances where each partner is the inversion of the other, in tango the language can be symmetrical, a symbolic equivalency that demands not identity but coordination. The common axis exists so that the couple does not lose its balance, but there are also two independent lanes in which each dancer can improvise.

This is shown, in the first step of this couple's choreography, in which the conditions of the dance are established: "Either we hold each other up and coordinate our movements or we won't be able to dance," the dancers say to each other in their gazes of recognition. But this simplicity requires an enormous amount of prior work: first, knowing themselves well enough to know which types of love they want and which they do not want (work unnecessary for those who prefer to believe in the power of love); later, renouncing the vices learned in previous embraces (intrigues, tricks, emotional games they've used successfully in the fields of the world of power.)

Without this knowledge and this unlearning it is impossible to evaluate priorities, and herein lays a key to the precise embrace. These women have discovered that the completeness their mothers never obtained, and which we therefore converted into a mandate for them, does not exist. No one can calm all their doubts; no one can save them for all time. These women have discovered that completeness is possible but in another way than they thought: rather than a form of totality, it is a way of precisely prioritizing emotional needs and vital desires. Someone could allow them all questions; someone could accompany them always in this process.

Andrés, a French sociologist the age of my daughters who works in the academic world, tries to explain what he wants from a woman he recognizes as similar to himself: "The attempt to resist the temptation to play a well-known game. Difficulty in absenting oneself. A game of hunters, of players, two hunters, two players. It's very hard to change the rules. Now, another game: a game of adults, between adults, played in a very different terrain, on another temporal scale, one of continuous time rather than static time. A game to be built, a deep game, between people ready to recognize each other and adventure and bare their souls and experiment and live fully. A marvelous unique game. Hard to find the right counterpart. Many never do. They find substitutes, people who resemble the counterparts but without taste or pleasure."

Carolina, a young Italian woman who works in the fashion world in New York, declines the offer: "I never imagined that I could meet someone like you. You're all I imagined in a man and more. But I can't stay with you. This love interests me, but not so strongly. I believe in lightness of being."

A tango professional is distinguished from a beginner because he does not need to make an effort. He feels comfortable, light. He and his partner glide around the dance floor like expert trapeze artists: ethereal, light and enviably comfortable in their difficult pirouettes. By contrast, the apprentice dancer needs to resort to clumsy gestures. His hand bothers her back, her arm rests too heavily on his shoulder; both seem to clump through the steps without any grace.

Carolina is right: the first moments of a love seeking the precise embrace are arduous, forced and awkward. Both dancers are more concerned with not making a misstep and with showing how much care and dedication they are ready to invest to learn how to love with precision than with enjoying the dance itself. But in rejecting Andrés as a beginner, she has also lost a unique opportunity to help him become an expert.

Andrés is disappointed, but he also emerges pleased because he has salvaged the most important part of this first step: for the first time in his romantic life, someone has understood what good of love he is looking for. "A thousand countries. A thousand nights. Hundreds of women. Seeking without stopping, without limits. The woman who both gives and lets herself receive affection doesn't exist. Or the women who fascinates and lets herself be fascinated. The woman who seduces and lets herself be seduced. Who is intelligent but lets herself be taught. Who flies and who lets me fly. I should accept the fact that she doesn't exist. But she does—I met her, I touched her. I know the love I want exists. I know I shouldn't stop looking. She didn't give me her love but she gave me confidence in my love."

Why didn't this encounter last? Because Carolina could only give herself to him and feel feminine in private, away from the public gaze. But she considered him insufficiently masculine—

he didn't belong to the right social class, he didn't dress, speak or think like such a man—and he wouldn't be accepted by her family or her social community.

Andrés' proposal didn't find an echo in Carolina. They could not emerge from limbo and invent together a new modality of being. But the gazes with whom they looked at each other let each understand better his own difficulties in loving and being loved as they wish.

In tango, the man leads and, if he is a good dancer, takes care neither to impede nor to dominate the woman. She completes the step with a symmetrical protagonism: it is the most she can do while also making sure not to continue until she receives the man's cue, because if she moves ahead without him she may lose her balance. If formerly the man led the dance in order to flaunt his woman, in a scene infused with *machismo*, the contemporary tango does not suffer these divisions of power. She no longer supports herself like deadweight on the mobile center of the man's steps; many steps previously scorned as feminine are now part of the man's repertoire.

Similarly, the second step of this new romantic choreography consists in the dancers' recognition of how they can help each other reveal themselves to the world without masks. As they are autodidacts, they lack maps and they fear becoming confused, not knowing how to discriminate between loving strangely and loving poorly; when their strangeness is brave and when frightening, when they guide and when they dominate, when they are progressing and when losing their balance. Emotional syncretes have come through a long process of self-acceptance and they have a fair idea of the complexities that make them who they are. They know the paradoxes of their internal angels and devils and above all they know that they don't want to renounce any of their component parts.

The dance partner who can help them is the one who functions as teacher, student, audience and director of the new, strange, different love scenes in which they want to play.

They need a partner who criticizes with strength and rigor but who also nurtures with goodness. They need a witness both rigorous in his impartiality and unconditional in his interest. They need an associate fair in his capacity to think and generous in his capacity to feel. They need the precise embrace.

This is very little and at the same time very much. Little because, once they can count on the critique, witness and support of the other in the presentation of their strange selves to the world, emotional syncretes can and want to complete this task without outside interference. Much because it is very hard for them to find a trustworthy partner, someone before whom they can show themselves as they are. They risk confirming the substance of the condemnatory glances they have received since their childhoods: if they discover fear in the other's eyes, they may feel crazier, sicker or worse than before; they will again fear themselves. But if they win, they will obtain what they have always wished for: the precise embrace that will let them enjoy their strangeness.

Such enjoyment is impossible if emotional needs are not reciprocal and reciprocally tended to. The interlocutory space that brings happiness to these people is so difficult to find, so gratuitous and at the same time so necessary that when they find it they know that it deserves the utmost care or, better said, the only care required by a partner: equivalency, the giving to the other of the same understanding of his strangeness as one claims for oneself. This reciprocity makes the precise embrace possible: mutually, the partners help each other to calm the fears of the little angel scared by the erupting rage of the little devil inside each. They look at each other mutually in the crisscrossed mirrors of their type.

"The tango pair interlaces its legs and makes its bodies bend at the same time, which requires symmetry between the dancer who leads and the partner who follows, as if they were completely united," Martin says in *El tango sempiterno*. For this reason this dance results in an expression equally feminine and masculine. "The embrace is equitable," Martin says, "it does not subjugate the woman, but exteriorizes the strength of both partners in the embrace; and when the bodies separate, the man is not the leader of but the mirror for the woman." This idea goes well beyond that of the vindication of improbable equalities, and lets one understand that joint love is based on emotional accountabilities that seek rigorous and discerning equivalencies. The partners seek symmetry and equivalency, rather than homogeneity.

Who's following whom? With this question, the syncretes come to the third step in the choreography. No one is identical to anyone else but some establish between themselves parallel, symmetrical, or equitable positions. If two dancers try to put the same foot in the same place at the same moment, they will both lose their balance and fall. Even if they don't fall, the dance will lose the grace, elegance, and comfort that emanate from harmoniously coordinated movements. If they think they must give each other exactly *the same* thing; they cannot dance this dance. To wash the same number of dishes, to earn the same amount of money, to caress each other the same number of times or to say *I love you* the same number of times may result in an egalitarian couple but also in a relationship unjust to and unsatisfying for both. Because the act of tallying and of making identical the needs, desires, and personal characteristics of both dancers means to limit them, to imprison them, to force them to fit into a mold that denies them any possibility of spontaneity or creativity. To erase difference and to negotiate relationships in order to equalize them negates the fact that no human being is identical to any other and condemns the participants to a boring, monotonous, shallow life. The pacts between people who seek just relationships by trying to transform themselves into identical beings end by impoverishing and creating resentment in both partners.

For those who learned to succeed playing the game of love of power, it's difficult to understand that a mutually chosen dependency is a gesture of autonomy rather than of submission, that an independence mutually planned is neither rebellion nor abandonment but liberty, that two people can do what the other wants while doing what they themselves want. But in my daughters' generation, there are some who understand this. If their grandmothers said *we* when they meant to say *I*, because there existed only a collective called family, their mothers broke that *we* in order to rescue the *I*. But the syncretes have accomplished much more: they have established an *I* capacious enough to include a *we*. They don't feel the panic of some contradictory women who fuse with the other and fear disappearing; rather, they incorporate the others into their own needs, so that acting on their own behalf means also acting on the other's behalf.

A skilled tangoist doesn't demand that the other be guided by what he does, but that the other is guided by the music. Those women who are strong but also good and those men who are good but not weak, women and men who attract one another, understand this manner of being in a relationship. They know that, precisely because they are equally strong, they can be equally good.

Here is one of these women writing to her partner: "Since our last phone call, I felt again that exultant feeling of freedom that I only feel with you. You liberate me. You take me to a place where I feel I can express myself, say what I think without filters, strategies, or fear. You make me feel more myself. It might strike you as strange that I content myself with so little: I only ask that you hug me. But your hug is more than essential for me: it permits me to make peace with myself. In your arms I find my home. Some men have offered me financial security and protection in order to start a family. Some have even offered me love. But none knew how to give me the liberty to be myself. So to bind myself to you aren't a sacrifice I'm making because I love you but a present I give myself out of self-love."

And his response: "Your hug also is essential for me. With you, I feel that I'm living out ideas that have fascinated me: Spinoza's theory, today rediscovered by neurobiology, but that I never understood as so practical. Spinoza writes about the importance of feelings in rational conduct, a position much more realistic and useful than the Cartesian position universally adopted by science. Something like adding "I feel, therefore I am" to the "I think, therefore I am." To do so lead by your hand is a gift given me by life."

The fourth step in the choreography requires the unlearning of the desire to compete in order to triumph over the other and the replacement of this notion by the desire to gain excellence by surpassing oneself. It is no longer about conquering the other, about destroying his will and making him say yes despite his own desires; it is about acquiring empathy, incorporating the desires and needs of the other into the encounter to which both are party. In this emotional territory, there exist neither conquerors nor conquered.

Vernon Castle, the early twentieth century dancer and teacher *extraordinaire*, writes of the tango that this silent dance "lets one concentrate the attention on the music and the lyrics" and that the beauty of the movements is valued more than that of the dancers. This lack of attention to the dancers themselves is important; those who dance this emotional encounter don't talk among themselves, but rather create a collectivity that encompasses both of them, the beauty of the movements, and the dialogue and incorporates that whole into another, greater whole, that of the music and the lyrics. They will know if they are dancing well or poorly via the partner, when they make a false step and squash the other's foot, but this correct or incorrect placement will happen as a function of the music, or, in other words, of the ethics of the emotional encounter.

In tango, the dancers support one another. The support comes from maintaining one's own axis, the woman in order to indicate and to follow, the man in order to guide and to lead. The dancers' profiles and faces are mutually supported, as are their torsos, but their legs and feet are free to go where they will. Thus each dancer completes his steps: alone, and accompanied. Neither could perform the figure of eight, the scissors, or any of the moves that make tango so rich if the other didn't support him. Each one concentrates on himself, listening to the inner music and adjusting his step accordingly, in order for the other to adjust his step. The pleasure of being in tune with this inner music guides, the idiosyncratic character of the choreography created by each couple.

In joint loves, each partner functions as well as a necessary support for the other's expression of himself. This choreography arranges itself into three parts: first, the two parts of the couple share a way of understanding love; second, they inform themselves—with meticulous precision—of the variations of feeling, desire, and needs of the other; and third, they trust in the creative and personal forms in which each expresses the same ideology of love.

The similarities in their ideas about love begin in the rejections of all that they do not want: they do not believe that they must negotiate the balance of power between themselves; they do not seek to take turns in being more visible in the world; they do not seek to make either sacrifices or compensatory gestures for those sacrifices. Whether still or in motion, the dancers take pleasure in a step well executed, that is to say, with excellence, generosity, and precision. Both share the leader's position because the love scene in which they play belongs to both jointly rather than to either separately. For both will the pleasure accrue; for both, the applause; for both, the pain, in case of failure or mistake.

Mutual information makes possible both the tango and the love. At the start, the search for precision can result in a suffocating practice: the dancers need to communicate their intentions to one another all the time and with a care for details that is almost obsessive. The apprenticeship to the tango is marked by too many gestures, too many choreographic novelties; that to the precise embrace, by too many words, too many ethical quandaries. Those who overcome this phase transform these quandaries into habits that need no thought: imperceptible gestures that inform one another of what they want, where they want to go, what steps they need to take. An utter intellectual rigor and an absolute transparency in intentions (of where one wants to go, in the tango) or of what one feels (in love) are required here. To know where the other is located allows for grace and elegance, without disturbance.

In tango as in love, it often happens that one partner cannot contain the almost atavistic desire to seize the initiative and to start or stop the movement without respect for the predetermined choreography. This partner lets himself be carried away by public demands and forgets that the steps are not his alone. He forgets that his virtuosity flourishes only in the presence of the other; he forgets that some excellence (*this* excellence) is achieved only in partnership or not at all. But only the precise embrace of the partner can help him to understand when his strangenesses are scary and when valuable, when to renounce them and when to cultivate them, when they are defensive reactions and when original ways of being.

Only when the minds think in unison, when hearts beat in unison, and when the dancers maintain themselves informed of these respective thoughts and feelings, is a motion possible that coordinates two sets of liberties and that follows the music of this new choreography of love. Just as in tango, the feet and legs are at liberty, it is not necessary for the dancers to control one another, to watch one another's movements, to ferret out each other's intentions. Each knows that the other seeks excellence and perfection in himself; each knows that this longing is based neither in narcissism and competition nor in lack of sociability. "He who does not desire excellence, who thinks that he does not deserve as much or does not dare to reach for as much, does not love himself enough," says Fernando Savater. And, one can add, that person will not know how to love sufficiently a syncrete, a person hard to love precisely, hard to approach and to understand in his astounding complexity.

The fifth step permits the dancers to develop their vital interests. As in tango, if the life partners trust one another, their steps become quick and agile. Each enters and leaves familiar places and there finds unfamiliar ones; together they improvise new postures, they play and they enjoy one another. They take pleasure in their shared liberty. Two versions of one dance, two versions of marking the same rhythm, two steps that join to form one, the coordination of difference.

The precise embrace doesn't promise the absence of bitterness implied by equality nor the absolute agreement impossible to effect between people. It offers and asks for the ability to harmoniously resolve the tension created by differences of position, point of view, and perspective of two people who want, simply, to love and to be loved. This choreography isn't based on a false identity but on true symmetry between the members of the couple. In life, as in the tango, the partners face each other, find one another, and support one another from positions equidistant to the axis formed by the intercalation of their two selves.

Slowly, then, and softly, they take the floor. The dancers seek symmetry: only when the other is equal in strength and nurturance but different in his manner of articulating these things can one find the richness of exchanging thoughts, feelings, and information.

Laura says: "I give the image of a strong woman, but I have always felt like a loser. Let's say I have a good of social shame that makes it hard for me to go out into the world and compete. Maybe it's not visible, but I feel that I never take the easiest path, that I always complicate things for myself. So it's hard for me to understand that Nicolas wants to be with me. So hard to understand that I literally didn't know why he called me the second time we went out. He had a million girlfriends, he was a known director at twenty-five, he spoke five languages—but he didn't know how to be intimate. I think that each can teach the other what is hard for him or unknown to him. We're attracted to what the other has that we lack."

The dancers promise to commit themselves to a common creation. They believe that a joint love is more than the sum of its parts and that its beauty consists in making clear its oddities to help them to resolve the tensions caused by the various conflicting needs within themselves. To avoid misunderstandings, these dancers don't pretend to be perfect. Instead, they try to be clear. They may make mistakes. But they take full responsibility for the avoidance of such. As *tangueros* are led by the music, these new women and men are led by truth.

The sixth step, in addition to practicing the love of truth, consists of a dialogue between the dancers' contradictions. There is no standard here, no blueprint: each embrace is particular and concrete, based on the infantile landscapes in which each member of the couple grew up. Although the partners feel joined in their strangeness, conflict and contradiction still differ from person to person. Dependence and independence, fusion and individuation, predictability and unpredictability, politeness and frankness, pragmaticism and idealism jostle with each other differently in different people. One may be strong in the economic sphere but weak in the social, good in the emotional plane but bad in the sexual. The variations in the internal dialogues of the dances are infinite.

It may happen that two people practicing this same new ethics of love find that they are not compatible with one another in an everyday love relationship. Those who are so compatible complement each other; each may lead, each may follow, now accepting, now questioning, without putting a stop to the joint learning to which both people have committed themselves. In the end there are no fixed rules.

They do not negotiate the balance of power, cede territory, nor share differences: they do not conform to one another, resignedly, dancing at the level that defines one of them alone. Their shared commitment to truth requires them to leave the floor, taking care of themselves by doing so, if despite their efforts they find they are incompatible.

These people don't seek self-awareness in order to float in introspective solipsism; they don't lose themselves by gazing fixedly at their own image like Narcissus. They want to know themselves in order to be better prepared for life, for the threatening thrill of the world, for its constant changes. For these people, love is an exit as well as an entrance: a way into the world as well as a way out.

Alessandra—the Italian lawyer found the embrace she ambitioned—says: "Neither of us can stand the other being in all our business. I don't understand these little couples who do everything together, as if they didn't have their own lives, as if they're afraid that the other will vanish if they go away for a minute. As long as I've been able to think, I've always had to have a secret. I don't keep a card up my sleeve—I need him to trust me without controlling me. And my husband needs the same. That I don't know what he's doing every minute doesn't mean that he takes advantage of the time to do something that would harm both of us. Our relationship is so special that it's not worth troubling it with lovers, although the freedom we give each other would let us do so."

Alessandra and other women (and some men) of my daughters' generation have brought to the emotional sphere some ideas about responsibility that originated in the professional sphere: the evaluation of the work's quality rather than of its duration or the force it took to do it; giving the best of themselves for the good of the work; asking to be paid according to what the work is worth. In these same ways they want to live their emotional lives: fulfilling their parts in a contract of love. They neither ask for nor offer a total embrace.

Those who enter into this new contract know that they need not agree about everything; they agree to disagree in order to continue the encounter.

So there are for the syncretes six steps. Nimble after years of hard work, they leave behind the drudgery of dichotomous thinking. Self-accepting after years of self-doubt, they leave behind the burning brands of conformist opinion. So the dance continues as the partners agree to the emotional contract, not once and in a stable way, but again and again in fluidity: led by truth, neither conquering nor being conquered, these daughters (and sons) of contradictory mothers strive towards lightness, towards gracefulness. In so doing, they teach us, their mothers, how to love.

I don't yet know much about what happened to my consultants after they found their romantic partners and joined them in the development of their respective precise embraces. Little time, two or three years at most, has passed since these women began to dance to the rhythm of the love of truth. Not enough time, in other words, to evaluate the prospects of a romantic project. Nevertheless, it's worth noting that the first experiences are encouraging and that some women have stopped seeing me because the emotional conflict that brought them to me has been resolved. In these cases, I trust that in romantic chronicles, as in life, no news is good news: when complex people can savor the happiness of perceiving themselves and perceiving others without fear, they do with complete dedication to the (joyful) task. They do not have time for testifying.

ACKNOWLEDGEMENTS

Some thanks are in the key of limbo. Save for Natasha and Paula, with whom I maintain a relationship that is the same internally and externally, I call those people who have helped me understand the manner of loving of emotional syncretes by those names with which I refer to them privately, inside. These names refer not to an external reality but to an internal one, and so I respect the privacy of the people to whom they belong.

My Mary Magdalene taught me that the virtuous are those who decide not to sin while knowing themselves capable of doing so, rather than those who have never entertained a stray sinful thought. With her I learned too that the brave are those who face their fears with steeliness and determination, rather than those who do not feel fear.

My Deborah the Judge taught me that the Hebrew words for "man" and "woman," when stripped of the two letters that differentiate them, result in the word for "fire." She taught me too that the letters so taken away, when recombined, form one way of referring to God in the Jewish tradition. And that the ways of reverencing truth are infinite.

My Ruth the Moabite taught me that sometimes one must disobey the letter of loved ones' mandates in order to obey fully and deeply their spirit. I also learned from her and her partner in navigation that taking oneself too seriously is as bad as not committing oneself seriously to others.

My Little Red Riding Hood got lost on the beach searching for sea snails, one day when she was three years old. When her

211

mother found her, she covered her with kisses and slaps, with cries of love and of fear; she told the girl she was bad for having gotten lost. From this daughter I learned that we mothers, when we feel guilty for not properly looking after our daughters, transfer to them the responsibility and make them feel guilty for not looking after us. I learned too that, in order not to lose oneself, the solution is not to give up curiosity or pleasure in treasure-hunting. Instead, the mother (inside oneself) should accompany the child (inside oneself), making sure the child does not get lost during excursions.

My Artemis the Huntress taught me that it is better to fight out of love than to refuse to fight out of indifference. I learned as well from her and her little girl that the first relationship to be established—for good or for bad—is with one's mother. The maternal relationship is primary.

My Sleeping Beauty taught me that it's difficult to leave one's limbo, that secure and trustworthy place, without the presence of someone outside oneself who makes the effort to try to understand the language of the person inside.

My Don Quixote taught me that ethics chart the course of those who navigate without cartographies or compasses. I also learned from him and his partner in navigation that, because appearances deceive, one should always look twice: one can be good and appear bad, or be bad and appear good.

My private Hermes taught me that there are loves that kill and distances that cure; there are embraces that stifle and blows that resurrect. I also learned from him that the best is the enemy of the good.

My private Confucius taught me that softness can be masculine as well as feminine and that patience is the gift received by those who learn how to be patient. He and his partner in navigation also taught me that a good deal benefits all involved.

My hardhearted dancer taught me that the pleasure and pain of dancing a *pas de deux* are inextricably intertwined. I also learned from him that there is no way of comparing the pleasure of dancing with a partner equally interested in reaching the most possible of perfections for that partnership.

My two shooting stars, not related to each other, taught me that one's own intuitions are an extraordinary source of information, especially if one learns how to differentiate them from tempestuous desires and uncontrollable impulses.

When she was little, Natasha insisted that her grandmothers dance because, she explained to them, that was the only way of not shriveling up. And her grandmothers rejuvenated themselves dancing dances she had invented. With her I learned that, if one knows how to accompany the rhythm, if one knows how to listen, one can dance any dance. A young woman who has not yet learned this lesson says: "I want to be a chameleon so I can resemble a geisha, a queen, a warrior, a prostitute, and in this way my boyfriend will never look at another woman." With Natasha, I learned that truth lives in the opposite idea: if one knows one's own local language perfectly, one can understand every language in the world.

With Natasha and Carlos, I learned that one must be very precise in one's expression of emotions so as not to drown in the chasm of couplehood. They taught me that sacred marriages are those that conjoin difference while separating similarity: the masculine and the feminine, feelings and thoughts, the personal and the communal, the past and the future, the private and the social, strength and goodness.

Paula taught me that those who tolerate the silence and solitude that accompany navigations through uncharted waters also possess the courage to make mistakes along the oath of the search for truth. My most profound gratitude goes to her, also, because she helped me to forgive myself: she insists that if I had not cleared new paths (as I could, violently, and with blows) in life, she would not have been able to travel along them with the tenderness and softness that are characteristic of her.

In the zone of translation between limbo and the outside world, thanks go to those whom I call by their own names.

Juan Manuel Obarrio, teacher and student, helped me conjoin thoughts and feelings.

Marcela Goglio, Gene Liebel and Valeria Biagosch, collaborators beyond any price, gave me the gift of their intimacy.

Saumya Ramarao, adopted daughter and companion in migration, helped me understand that men and women in all parts of the world and in different languages, traditions, tastes, scents and colors share the longing to understand and to be understood; to embrace and to be embraced; to love and to be loved, at once.

Mercedes Pardo, disciple and friend, believed in me so much that I became able to believe in myself and to sustain myself in those moments when I didn't remember why or for whom I was writing this book.

Silvia Galperin and Edna Soter, colleagues and friends, with their affection and understanding, helped me move through one of the most fruitful but also painful moments of my life.

In the outside world, because they do not know how important they were for me, I thank four people who in my imagination worked as parental figures. With masculine tenderness, Jerome Brunner critiqued my first writings. In the same period, Luisa Valenzuela praised my ideas—leaving out her comments about the form of their expression—with feminine strength. Years later, Juan Carlos Kreimer demanded more rigor in the book's definition, while Isabel Toyos applauded various versions of the chapters. To paraphrase Winicott, these two women helped the book to exist while these two men encouraged me to build this book. None is responsible for any part of the content.

Gabriela Esquivada and Liana Scalettar helped me to translate myself. Without them, this book would not have emerged from my limbo.

Valeria Solomonoff, tango expert, was precise—better than perfect—in her explanations of choreography. The responsibility for the ways in which I've used tango as a metaphor is entirely my own.

Juliana Neiman listened with attention and love the last versions of this book. I can always count on her ever present and multifaceted attention.

Bibi Calderaro exercised her bilingualism, as well as her patience, in the laborious comparison between the Spanish and English versions.

María Teresa and Enrique Rodriguez Boulán gave me shelter many weekends in their Quogue home, where I wrote most of this book. Their trustworthy and generous hospitality allows everybody to feel at home.

I cannot find the words necessary to thank properly my sister and brother, my brother-in-law and my ex-sister-in-law, my niece and her partner, my nephews and their partners, my aunts and uncles who—sometimes voluntarily and sometimes involuntarily—allowed me to watch them as they lived and loved.

It is left to me to say that, thanks to my daughters, I learned how to savor joint loves. Too late to do so with their father, but in time to do so with Jorge, the good man whom I rejected when I feared destroying him with my badness. During their childhoods and adolescences, the girls taught me enough to know that, if I wanted to—if I recovered my goodness, then trapped in ancestral rage that made me fear feeling inferior for having been born female—I could also be deserving of a joint love with a good man.

> *O terceiro me chegou com que chega do nada*
> *Ele não me trouxe nada tambem nada perguntou*
> *Mal sei como ele se chama mas entendo o que ele quer*
> *Se deitou na minha cama e me chama de muher*
> *Foi chegando sorrateiro e antes que eu dissesse não*
> *Se instalou feito um posseiro dentro de meu coração.*

> (The third one came to me as if coming from nowhere
> He brought me nothing, asked me nothing
> I barely know his name but understand his desire
> He lay down on my bed and called me woman
> He approached me surreptitiously and before I could
>   say no
> He settled without doubting in the middle of my heart).

Twenty years after I rejected Jorge because I thought he was weak, we met again. During the time in which we knew nothing of one another, Jorge had abandoned his fear of being bad and had learned how to defend himself—with emotional strength recovered from the ancestral guilt caused him by the fear of feeling superior for having been born male—from strong women like me. And for twenty years now we have enjoyed teaching each other what our devils and angels want, with strength and goodness, as Natasha and Paula showed me it was possible to do. In limbo, apart from him, and in the complex transitions between limbo and the outside world, Jorge always gives me a precise embrace.

BIBLIOGRAPHY

I include here only those books that, having touched me most personally, relate to the problematic which I write about in this book. They are: *La llama doble*, by Octavio Paz; *Psyche and Eros*, by Gisella Labouvie-Vieff; *Traces*, by Niki de Saint Phalle; *La ética como amor propio*, by Fernando Savater; *Love is a story*, by Robert Steinberg; *What our mothers didn't tell us*, by Danielle Crittenden; *The normal chaos of love*; by Ulrich Beck and Elisabeth Beck-Gernsheim; *Fausse route*, by Elisabeth Badinter; *The transformation of intimacy*, by Anthony Giddens. And also three songs: *Terezinha*, by Chico Buarque; *Começar de novo*, by Ivan Lins and Vitor Martins, and *Cambalache*, by Enrique Santos Discépolo.